I0023177

George Washington

Rules of Conduct

Diary of Adventure, Letters, and Farewell Addresses

George Washington

Rules of Conduct
Diary of Adventure, Letters, and Farewell Addresses

ISBN/EAN: 9783744700528

Printed in Europe, USA, Canada, Australia, Japan

Cover: Foto ©Suzi / pixelio.de

More available books at **www.hansebooks.com**

The Riverside Literature Series

RULES OF CONDUCT

DIARY OF ADVENTURE, LETTERS, AND FAREWELL ADDRESSES

BY

GEORGE WASHINGTON

WITH INTRODUCTIONS AND NOTES

HOUGHTON, MIFFLIN AND COMPANY
Boston: 4 Park Street; New York: 11 East Seventeenth Street
Chicago: 378-388 Wabash Avenue
The Riverside Press, Cambridge

The Riverside Press, Cambridge, Mass., U. S. A.
Electrotyped and Printed by H. O. Houghton & Company.

PREFACE.

THERE are many biographies of Washington, and every history of the United States gives prominence to the facts in the life of the great leader in the war for independence, and the first President of the Union. The city where the Congress of the nation meets is named after the greatest American, and every year on the twenty-second of February the people are given a holiday to remind them of the man whose birth meant so much to the nation. It is of prime importance that a democracy, which recognizes the worth of the person, has for its great exemplar a man so wise, so noble, so unselfish as its first citizen. Character makes character, and the figure of Washington as it looms up in the past is a rebuke to all that is mean and ignoble in American public life.

The birthday of Washington, coming in the middle of winter, offers a capital opportunity for schools to take a little rest and enjoy a special celebration. This pamphlet gives in convenient form the most striking passages in Washington's life, told in his own words, with such preliminary notes as are needed to make the circumstances of the writing clear. There is material, therefore, for a celebration, and by a little ingenuity it can be used in a variety of ways. Thus, as part of the exercises, each member of the class may choose one of the rules to recite and to take as a motto for practical conduct. If the school is situated near any point visited by Washington, some one of the scholars may prepare an essay upon the local associations with Washington, or there may be a written newspaper, edited by one of the class, and containing contributions from various members. It will often be possible to borrow from some museum in the neighborhood the dress of a continental soldier to use in an effective tableau.

Mr. Lowell's poem, "Under the Old Elm," has some noble lines characterizing Washington. The fact that Longfellow's home was the headquarters originally of Washington in Cambridge, gives an opportunity for a pleasing connection between the statesman and the poet. As Washington is so closely identified with the war for independence, the children may be encouraged to bring in revolutionary relics, and a temporary museum can be made with talks about the different objects. Even if nothing else is done, this little volume can be read by turns in the class, and a geographical exercise connected with it.

CONTENTS.

WASHINGTON'S RULES.

THE copy-books and exercise-books of most boys are early destroyed, but it chances that those of George Washington have been kept, and they are very interesting. The handwriting in them is the first thing to be noticed, — round, fair, and bold, the letters large like the hand that formed them, and the lines running straight and even. In the arithmetic and book-keeping manuals which we study at school, there are printed forms of receipts, bills, and other ordinary business papers ; but in Washington's school-days, the teacher showed the boys how to draw these up, and gave them also copies of longer papers, like leases, deeds, and wills. There were few lawyers in Virginia, and every gentleman was supposed to know many forms of documents which now are left to our lawyers or stationers.

Washington's exercise-books have many pages of these forms, written out carefully by the boy. Sometimes he made ornamental letters such as clerks were wont to use. This was not merely exercise in penmanship ; it was practice work in all that careful keeping of accounts and those business methods which were sure to be needed by one who had to manage a large plantation. George Washington was to manage something greater, though no one then knew it ; and the habits which he formed at this time were of inestimable value to him in his manhood.

The manuscript book which contains these exercises has also a list of a hundred and ten *Rules of Civility and Decent Behavior in Company and Conversation*. They were probably not made up by the boy, but copied from some book, or taken down from the lips of his mother or teacher. Fifty-seven of them are printed by Mr. Sparks in his *Writings of Washington*. They sound rather stiff to us, but it was a common thing in those days to set such rules before children, and George Washington, with his liking for regular, orderly ways — evident in his very writing — probably used the rules and perhaps committed them to memory, to secure an even temper and self-control. They touch on things great and small. The difficulty with most boys would be to follow a hundred and ten of such rules. They serve, however, to show what was the standard of good manners and morals among those who had the training of George Washington. The best of rules would have done little with poor stuff; it was because this boy had a manly and honorable spirit that he could be trained in manly and honorable ways.

1. Every action in company ought to be with some sign of respect to those present.

2. In the presence of others sing not to yourself with a humming noise, nor drum with your fingers or feet.

3. Sleep not when others speak, sit not when others stand, speak not when you should hold your peace, walk not when others stop.

4. Turn not your back to others, especially in speaking; jog not the table or desk on which another reads or writes; lean not on any one.

5. Be no flatterer; neither play with any one that delights not to be played with.

6. Read no letters, books, or papers in company; but when there is a necessity for doing it, you must ask leave. Come not near the books or writings of any one so as to read them, unless desired, nor give your opinion of them unasked; also, look not nigh when another is writing a letter.

7. Let your countenance be pleasant, but in serious matters somewhat grave.

8. Show not yourself glad at the misfortune of another, though he were your enemy.

9. When you meet with one of greater quality than yourself, stop and retire, especially if it be at a door or any strait place, to give way for him to pass.

10. They that are in dignity, or in office, have in all places precedency; but whilst they are young they ought to respect those that are their equals in birth or other qualities, though they have no public charge.

11. It is good manners to prefer them to whom we speak before ourselves, especially if they be above us with whom in no sort we ought to begin.

12. Let your discourse with men of business be short and comprehensive.

13. In visiting the sick, do not presently play the physician if you be not knowing therein.

14. In writing, or speaking, give to every person his due title, according to his degree and the custom of the place.

15. Strive not with your superiors in argument, but always submit your judgment to others with modesty.

16. Undertake not to teach your equal in the art himself professes: it savors of arrogancy.

17. When a man does all he can, though it succeeds not well, blame not him that did it.

18. Being to advise, or reprehend any one, consider whether it ought to be in public or in private, presently or at some other time, and in what terms to do it; and in reproving show no signs of choler, but do it with sweetness and mildness.

19. Take all admonitions thankfully, in what time or place soever given; but afterwards, not being culpable, take a time and place convenient to let him know it that gave them.

20. Mock not, nor jest at anything of importance; break no jests that are sharp-biting, and if you deliver anything witty and pleasant, abstain from laughing thereat yourself.

21. Wherein you reprove another be unblamable

yourself; for example is more prevalent than precepts.

22. Use no reproachful language against any one, neither curse nor revile.

23. Be not hasty to believe flying reports to the disparagement of any.

24. In your apparel be modest, and endeavor to accommodate nature, rather than to procure admiration; keep to the fashion of your equals, such as are civil and orderly with respect to times and places.

25. Play not the peacock, looking everywhere about you to see if you be well decked, if your shoes fit well, if your stockings sit neatly, and clothes handsomely.

26. Associate yourself with men of good quality, if you esteem your own reputation, for it is better to be alone than in bad company.

27. Let your conversation be without malice or envy, for it is a sign of a tractable and commendable nature; and in all causes of passion, admit reason to govern.

28. Be not immodest in urging your friend to discover a secret.

29. Utter not base and frivolous things amongst grave and learned men; nor very difficult questions or subjects among the ignorant; nor things hard to be believed.

30. Speak not of doleful things in time of mirth, nor at the table; speak not of melancholy things, as death, and wounds, and if others mention them, change, if you can, the discourse. Tell not your dreams, but to your intimate friend.

31. Break not a jest where none takes pleasure in mirth; laugh not aloud, nor at all without occasion. Deride no man's misfortune, though there seem to be some cause.

32. Speak not injurious words, neither in jest nor earnest; scoff at none although they give occasion.

33. Be not forward, but friendly and courteous; the first to salute, hear, and answer; and be not pensive when it is a time to converse.

34. Detract not from others, neither be excessive in commending.

35. Go not thither where you know not whether you shall be welcome or not. Give not advice without being asked, and when desired, do it briefly.

36. If two contend together, take not the part of either unconstrained, and be not obstinate in your own opinion; in things indifferent be of the major side.

37. Reprehend not the imperfections of others, for that belongs to parents, masters, and superiors.

38. Gaze not on the marks or blemishes of others, and ask not how they came. What you may speak in secret to your friend, deliver not before others.

39. Speak not in an unknown tongue in company, but in your own language, and that as those of quality do and not as the vulgar; sublime matters treat seriously.

40. Think before you speak; pronounce not imperfectly, nor bring out your words too hastily, but orderly and distinctly.

41. When another speaks be attentive yourself, and disturb not the audience. If any hesitate in his words, help him not, nor prompt him without being desired; interrupt him not, nor answer him, till his speech be ended.

42. Treat with men at fit times about business: and whisper not in the company of others.

43. Make no comparisons, and if any of the company be commended for any brave act of virtue, commend not another for the same.

44. Be not apt to relate news if you know not the truth thereof. In discoursing of things you have heard, name not your author always. A secret discover not.

45. Be not curious to know the affairs of others, neither approach to those that speak in private.

46. Undertake not what you cannot perform, but be careful to keep your promise.

47. When you deliver a matter, do it without passion and with discretion, however mean the person be you do it to.

48. When your superiors talk to anybody, hearken not, neither speak, nor laugh.

49. In disputes be not so desirous to overcome as not to give liberty to each one to deliver his opinion, and submit to the judgment of the major part, especially if they are judges of the dispute.

50. Be not tedious in discourse ; make not many digressions, nor repeat often the same manner of discourse.

51. Speak not evil of the absent, for it is unjust.

52. Make no show of taking great delight in your victuals ; feed not with greediness ; cut your bread with a knife ; lean not on the table ; neither find fault with what you eat.

53. Be not angry at table, whatever happens, and if you have reason to be so, show it not ; put on a cheerful countenance, especially if there be strangers, for good humor makes one dish of meat a feast.

54. Set not yourself at the upper end of the table ; but if it be your due, or that the master of the house will have it so, contend not, lest you should trouble the company.

55. When you speak of God or his attributes, let it

be seriously in reverence. Honor and obey your natural parents, although they be poor.

56. Let your recreations be manful, not sinful.

57. Labor to keep alive in your breast that little spark of celestial fire, called conscience.

II.

A DANGEROUS ERRAND.

In 1753 the French and the English were both trying to get possession of the Valley of the Ohio, and news came to Virginia that the French governor of Canada had sent troops and supplies into the country, was making friends with the Indians, and had even seized certain English traders and sent them prisoners to France. The English people most directly interested in the matter were the members of the Ohio Company, a land company formed for the purpose of occupying and settling what was vaguely known as the Ohio country, that is, the land watered by the Ohio River and its tributaries. The governor of Virginia was a stockholder in the company, and he determined at once to send a commissioner to the officer in command of the French forces, and ask by what right Frenchmen were building forts in the king's dominions, and what they were intending to do; why they had made prisoners of peaceable Englishmen; and as the two nations were not at war, why French soldiers were invading English territory. Moreover, the commissioner was to see the Indian chiefs and make sure that they did not form an alliance with the French.

It was no slight matter for any one to undertake such an errand. He must know something of the country; he must be used to the Indians; he must be a person whom the French would respect; above all, he must be strong of body, courageous, prudent, wise, and on the alert; for the journey would be a severe one, and the messenger would need to have what is called a "level head." Of course no one expected that the French commandant would kindly sit down and tell the Virginian commissioner what he meant to do; the commissioner must find that out by his own sagacity.

Now, one of the principal members of the Ohio Company was Lawrence Washington, who had recently died and left his affairs in the hands of his younger brother George. George Washington knew perfectly what interests were at stake. Besides, he was a backwoodsman; it was no novelty for him to follow trails through the forest; he could deal with Indians; and above all, he had shown himself a clear-headed, far-sighted young man, whom every one instinctively trusted. He was one of His Majesty's officers, for he was Adjutant-General of the Northern District, and so, though Major George Washington was but twenty-one years old, Governor Dinwiddie and his council selected him for this delicate and weighty mission.

It was no summer jaunt on which he set out. He waited upon the governor at Williamsburg, and was armed with papers duly signed and sealed with the great seal of Virginia, giving him authority as commissioner. On October 30, 1753, he left Williamsburg with a journey of more than a thousand miles before him. He stopped at Fredericksburg to say good-by to his mother, and to engage his old fencing-master, Van Braam, as an interpreter. Washington knew no French, and never learned it. Van Braam pretended to know it well, but really had only an ignorant smattering of the language. From Fredericksburg Washington went to Alexandria, where he laid in supplies, and to Winchester, which was the most important frontier settlement, where he provided himself with horses, tents, and other camp equipments.

The real start of the expedition was to be made from Wills Creek, now Cumberland, in Maryland, which was the outpost of civilization. Here Washington arrived November 14, and made up his little company. It consisted of Christopher Gist, who was in the employ of the Ohio Company and was an experienced frontiersman; Jacob Van Braam, the interpreter; Davidson, an Indian interpreter; and four frontiersmen. The party was now complete, and the next day plunged into the wilderness.

Washington kept a journal of this expedition, in which he set down his adventures. He had great difficulty in getting at the French commandant, but finally reached him at Fort Le Bœuf. The passages in the Journal which follow detail the experiences of Washington from this time till he returned to Williamsburg and made his report to the governor.

December 12. — I prepared early to wait upon the commander, and was received and conducted to him by the second officer in command. I acquainted him with my business, and offered my commission and letter; both of which he desired me to keep until the arrival of Monsieur Reparti, captain at the next fort, who was sent for and expected every hour.

This commander is a knight of the military order of St. Louis, and named Legardeur de St. Pierre. He is an elderly gentleman, and has much the air of a soldier. He was sent over to take the command immediately upon the death of the late general, and arrived here about seven days before me.

At two o'clock, the gentleman who was sent for arrived, when I offered the letter, etc. again, which they received, and adjourned into a private apartment for the captain to translate, who understood a little English. After he had done it, the commander desired I would walk in and bring my interpreter to peruse and correct it; which I did.

December 13. — The chief officers retired to hold a council of war, which gave me an opportunity of taking the dimensions of the fort, and making what observations I could.

It is situated on the south or west fork of French Creek, near the water; and is almost surrounded by the creek, and a small branch of it, which form a kind of island. Four houses compose the sides. The bastions are made of piles driven into the ground, standing more than twelve feet above it, and sharp at top, with port-holes cut for cannon, and loop-holes for the small arms to fire through. There are eight six-pounds pieces mounted in each bastion, and one piece of four pounds before the gate. In the bastions are a guard-house, chapel, doctor's lodging, and the commander's private store; round which are laid platforms for the cannon and men to stand on. There are several barracks without the fort, for the soldiers' dwellings, covered, some with bark, and some with boards, made chiefly of logs. There are also several other houses, such as stables, smith's shop, etc.

I could get no certain account of the number of men here; but, according to the best judgment I could form, there are a hundred, exclusive of officers, of whom there are many. I also gave orders to the people who were with me, to take an exact account of the canoes, which were hauled up to convey their forces down in the spring. This they did, and told fifty of the birch bark, and a hundred and seventy of pine; besides many others, which were blocked out, in readiness for being made.

December 14. — As the snow increased very fast, and our horses daily became weaker, I sent them off unloaded, under the care of Barnaby Currin and two others, to make all convenient dispatch to Venango,[1] and there to wait our arrival, if there was a prospect of the river's freezing; if not, then to continue down to Shannopin's Town, at the Fork of the Ohio, and there to wait until we came to cross the Allegany; intending myself to go down by water, as I had the offer of a canoe or two.

As I found many plots concerted to retard the Indians' business, and prevent their returning with me, I endeavored all that lay in my power to frustrate their schemes, and hurried them on to execute their intended design. They accordingly pressed for admittance this evening, which at length was granted them,

[1] Now Franklin, in Venango County, Pennsylvania.

privately, to the commander and one or two other officers. The Half-King[1] told me, that he offered the wampum to the commander, who evaded taking it, and made many fair promises of love and friendship; said he wanted to live in peace and trade amicably with them, as a proof of which he would send some goods immediately down to the Logstown[2] for them. But I rather think the design of that is to bring away all our straggling traders they meet with, as I privately understood they intended to carry an officer with them. And what rather confirms this opinion, I was inquiring of the commander by what authority he had made prisoners of several of our English subjects. He told me that the country belonged to them; that no Englishman had a right to trade upon those waters; and that he had orders to make every person prisoner, who attempted it on the Ohio, or the waters of it.

I inquired of Captain Reparti about the boy that was carried by this place, as it was done while the command devolved on him, between the death of the late general and the arrival of the present. He acknowledged that a boy had been carried past, and that the Indians had two or three white men's scalps (I was told by some of the Indians at Venango, eight), but pretended to have forgotten the name of the place where the boy came from, and all the particular facts, though he had questioned him for some hours, as they were carrying him past. I likewise inquired what they had done with John Trotter and James McClocklan, two Pennsylvania traders, whom they had taken with all their goods. They told me, that they had been sent to Canada, but were now returned home.

[1] The Half-King was an Indian chief, who with other Indians had joined Washington after he had entered the woods.

[2] On the Ohio River, about seventeen miles from Pittsburg.

This evening I received an answer to his Honor the Governor's letter from the commandant.

December 15. — The commandant ordered a plentiful store of liquor and provision to be put on board our canoes, and appeared to be extremely complaisant, though he was exerting every artifice which he could invent to set our Indians at variance with us, to prevent their going until after our departure; presents, rewards, and everything, which could be suggested by him or his officers. I cannot say that ever in my life I suffered so much anxiety as I did in this affair. I saw that every stratagem which the most fruitful brain could invent was practised to win the Half-King to their interest, and that leaving him there was giving them the opportunity they aimed at. I went to the Half-King and pressed him in the strongest terms to go; he told me that the commandant would not discharge him until the morning. I then went to the commandant and desired him to do their business, and complained of ill treatment; for keeping them, as they were part of my company, was detaining me. This he promised not to do, but to forward my journey as much as he could. He protested he did not keep them, but was ignorant of the cause of their stay; though I soon found it out. He had promised them a present of guns, if they would wait until the morning. As I was very much pressed by the Indians to wait this day for them, I consented, on a promise that nothing should hinder them in the morning.

December 16. — The French were not slack in their inventions to keep the Indians this day also. But as they were obliged, according to promise, to give the present, they then endeavored to try the power of liquor, which I doubt not would have prevailed at any other time than this; but I urged and insisted with the King so closely upon his word, that he refrained, and set off with us as he had engaged.

We had a tedious and very fatiguing passage down the creek. Several times we had like to have been staved against rocks; and many times were obliged all hands to get out and remain in the water half an hour or more, getting over the shoals. At one place, the ice had lodged, and made it impassable by water; we were, therefore, obliged to carry our canoe across the neck of land, a quarter of a mile over. We did not reach Venango until the 22d, where we met with our horses.

This creek is extremely crooked. I dare say the distance between the fort and Venango cannot be less than one hundred and thirty miles, to follow the meanders.

December 23. — When I got things ready to set off, I sent for the Half-King, to know whether he intended to go with us or by water. He told me that White Thunder had hurt himself much, and was sick and unable to walk; therefore he was obliged to carry him down in a canoe. As I found he intended to stay here a day or two, and knew that Monsieur Joncaire would employ every scheme to set him against the English, as he had before done, I told him, I hoped he would guard against his flattery, and let no fine speeches influence him in their favor. He desired I might not be concerned, for he knew the French too well for any thing to engage him in their favor; and that though he could not go down with us, he yet would endeavor to meet at the Fork with Joseph Campbell, to deliver a speech for me to carry to his

Honor the Governor. He told me he would order the Young Hunter to attend us, and get provisions, etc. if wanted.

Our horses were now so weak and feeble, and the baggage so heavy (as we were obliged to provide all the necessaries which the journey would require), that we doubted much their performing it. Therefore, myself and others, except the drivers, who were obliged to ride, gave up our horses for packs, to assist along with the baggage. I put myself in an Indian walking-dress, and continued with them three days, until I found there was no probability of their getting home in any reasonable time. The horses became less able to travel every day; the cold increased very fast; and the roads were becoming much worse by a deep snow, continually freezing; therefore, as I was uneasy to get back, to make report of my proceedings to his Honor the Governor, I determined to prosecute my journey, the nearest way through the woods, on foot.

Accordingly, I left Mr. Van Braam in charge of our baggage, with money and directions to provide necessaries from place to place for themselves and horses, and to make the most convenient dispatch in travelling.

I took my necessary papers, pulled off my clothes, and tied myself up in a watch-coat. Then, with gun in hand, and pack on my back, in which were my papers and provisions, I set out with Mr. Gist, fitted in the same manner, on Wednesday the 26th. The day following, just after we had passed a place called Murdering Town (where we intended to quit the path and steer across the country for Shannopin's Town), we fell in with a party of French Indians, who had lain in wait for us. One of them fired at Mr. Gist or me, not fifteen steps off, but fortunately missed. We took this fellow into custody, and kept him until about nine o'clock at night, then let him go, and walked all the remaining part of the night without making any stop, that we might get the start so far as to be out of the reach of their pursuit the next day, since we were well assured they would follow our track as soon as it was light. The next day we continued travelling until quite dark, and got to the river about two miles above Shannopin's. We expected to have found the river frozen, but it was not, only about fifty yards from each shore. The ice, I suppose, had broken up above, for it was driving in vast quantities.

There was no way for getting over but on a raft, which we set about, with but one poor hatchet, and finished just after sun-setting. This was a whole day's work; we next got it launched, then went on board of it, and set off; but before we were half-way over we were jammed in the ice, in such a manner that we expected every moment our raft to sink, and ourselves to perish. I put out my setting-pole to try to stop the raft, that the ice might pass by, when the rapidity of the stream threw it with so much violence against the pole that it jerked me out into ten feet water; but I fortunately saved myself by catching hold of one of the raft-logs. Notwithstanding all our efforts, we could not get to either shore, but were obliged, as we were near an island, to quit our raft and make to it.

The cold was so extremely severe, that Mr. Gist had all his fingers and some of his toes frozen, and the water was shut up so hard, that we found no difficulty in getting off the island on the ice in the morning, and went to Mr. Frazier's. We met here with twenty warriors, who were going to the southward to war; but coming to a place on the head of the Great Kenhawa, where they found seven people killed and scalped (all but one woman with very light hair), they turned about and ran back, for fear the inhabitants should rise and take them as the authors of the murder. They report that the bodies were lying about the house, and some of them much torn and eaten by the hogs. By the marks which were left, they say they were French Indians of the Ottawa nation, who did it.

As we intended to take horses here, and it required some time to find them, I went up about three miles to the mouth of Youghiogany, to visit Queen Aliquippa, who had expressed great concern that we passed her in going to the fort. I made her a present of a watch-coat and a bottle of rum, which latter was thought much the better present of the two.

Tuesday, the 1st of January, we left Mr. Frazier's house, and arrived at Mr. Gist's, at Monongahela, the 2d, where I bought a horse and saddle. The 6th, we met seventeen horses loaded with materials and stores for a fort at the Fork of the Ohio, and the day after, some families going out to settle. This day, we arrived at Wills Creek, after as fatiguing a journey as it is possible to conceive, rendered so by excessive bad weather. From the 1st day of December to the 15th there was but one day on which it did not rain or snow incessantly; and throughout the whole journey we met with nothing but one continued series of cold, wet weather, which occasioned very uncomfortable lodgings, especially after we had quitted our tent, which was some screen from the inclemency of it.

On the 11th, I got to Belvoir,[1] where I stopped one day to take necessary rest; and then set out and arrived in Williamsburg the 16th, where I waited upon his Honor the Governor, with the letter I had brought from the French commandant, and to give an account of the success of my proceedings. This I beg leave to do by offering the foregoing narrative, as it contains the most remarkable occurrences which happened in my journey.

I hope what has been said will be sufficient to make your Honor satisfied with my conduct; for that was my aim in undertaking the journey, and chief study throughout the prosecution of it.

III.

WITH GENERAL BRADDOCK.

Washington had been an officer in command of Virginia troops in the war between England and France, when, in February, 1755, General Braddock arrived in Virginia with two regiments of regular troops from England. Everybody expected that the French would at once be driven out of the Ohio valley, and General Braddock was one of the most confident. There was a bustle in every quarter, and Alexandria was made the headquarters from which troops, military stores, and provisions were to be sent forward, for they could be brought up to that point in men-of-war and transports.

As soon as Braddock had arrived in the country, Washington had addressed him a letter of welcome, and now he was keenly intent on the general's movements. From Mount Vernon he could see the ships in the Potomac and hear the din of preparation. He could not ride into town or to Belvoir without being

[1] A plantation belonging to the Fairfax family, not far from Mt. Vernon.

in the midst of the excitement. This was something very different from the poor, niggardly conduct of war which he had known in the colony. It was on a great scale; it was war carried on by His Majesty's troops, well clad, splendidly equipped and drilled, under the lead of a veteran general. He longed to join them. Here would be a chance such as he had never had, to learn something of the art of war; but he held no commission, and he had not even a company to offer. Nor was he willing to be a militia captain and subject to the orders of some lieutenant in the regular army.

He was considering how he might volunteer, when he received exactly the kind of invitation which he desired. He was a marked man now, and it did not take long for word to reach General Braddock that a young Virginian colonel, who had shown great spirit and ability in a recent expedition, and was thoroughly familiar with the route they were to take, desired to serve under him, but not as a subordinate captain. There was a way out of the difficulty, and the General at once invited Washington to join his military family as aid-de-camp. Washington joyfully accepted, and the following brief letters give a glimpse of his connection with the disastrous Braddock's Expedition, which set out with flags flying to capture Fort Duquesne, where Pittsburgh now stands, and was instead terribly defeated on the way. Robert Orme, to whom the first letter was written, was the aid-de-camp of Braddock who had informed Washington of his appointment.

I. TO ROBERT ORME.

MOUNT VERNON, 15 *March*, 1755.

SIR:

I was not favored with your polite letter, of the 2d instant, until yesterday; acquainting me with the notice his Excellency, General Braddock, is pleased to honor me with, by kindly inviting me to become one of his family the ensuing campaign. It is true, sir, I have, ever since I declined my late command, expressed an inclination to serve in this campaign as a volunteer; and this inclination is not a little increased, since it is likely to be conducted by a gentleman of the general's experience.

But, besides this, and the laudable desire I may have to serve with my best abilities my king and country, I must be ingenuous enough to confess, that I am not a little biased by selfish considerations. To explain, sir, I wish earnestly to attain some knowledge in the military profession, and, believing a more favorable opportunity cannot offer than to serve under a gentleman of General Braddock's abilities and experience, it does, you may reasonably suppose, not a little contribute to influence my choice. But, sir, as I have taken the liberty to express my sentiments so freely, I must beg your indulgence while I add, that the only bar which can check me in the pursuit of this object, is the inconveniences that must necessarily result from some proceedings, which happened a little before the general's arrival, and which, in some measure, had abated the ardor of my desires, and determined me to lead a life of retirement, into which I was just entering, at no small expense, when your favor was presented to me.

But, as I shall do myself the honor of waiting upon his Excellency as soon as I hear of his arrival at Alexandria, (I would do it sooner, were I certain where to find him,) I shall decline saying anything further on this head till then , begging you will be pleased to assure him, that I shall always retain a grateful sense of the favor with which he is pleased to honor me, and that I should have embraced this opportunity of writing to him, had I not recently addressed a congratulatory letter to him on his safe arrival in this country.

I flatter myself you will favor me in making a communication of these sentiments.

You do me a singular favor in proposing an acquaintance. It cannot but be attended with the most flattering prospects on my part, as you may already perceive by the familiarity and freedom with which I now enter upon this correspondence; a freedom which, even if it is disagreeable, you must excuse, and lay the blame of it at your own door, for encouraging me to throw off that restraint which otherwise might have been more obvious in my deportment on such an occasion.

The hope of shortly seeing you will be an excuse for my not adding more than that I shall endeavor to approve myself worthy of your friendship, and that I beg to be esteemed your most obedient servant.

II. TO JOHN ROBINSON, SPEAKER OF THE HOUSE OF DELEGATES, VIRGINIA.

MOUNT VERNON, 20 *April*, 1755.

DEAR SIR:

I little expected, when I wrote you last, that I should so soon engage in another campaign; but, in doing it, I may be allowed to claim some merit, if it is considered that the sole motive which invites me to the field is the laudable desire of serving my country, not the gratification of any ambitious or lucrative plans. This, I flatter myself, will manifestly appear by my going as a volunteer, without expectation of reward, or prospect of obtaining a command, as I am confidently assured it is not in General Braddock's power to give me a commission that I would accept. Perhaps by many others the above declaration might be construed into self-applause, which, unwilling to lose, I proclaim myself. But by you, sir, I expect it will be viewed in a different light, because you have sympathized in my disappointments, and lent your friendly aid to reinstate me in a suitable command; the recollection of which can never be lost upon a mind that is not insensible of obligations, but always ready to acknowledge them.

This is the reason why I am so much more unreserved, in the expression of my sentiments to you, than I should be to the world, whose censures and criticisms often place good designs in a bad light. But, to be ingenuous, I must confess I have other intentions in writing you this letter; for, if there is any merit in my case, I am unwilling to hazard it among my friends without this exposition of facts, as they might conceive that some advantageous offers had engaged my services, when, in reality, it is otherwise, for I expect to be a considerable loser in my private affairs by going. It is true I have been importuned to make this campaign by General Braddock as a member of his family, he conceiving, I suppose, that the small knowledge I have had an opportunity of acquiring of the country, Indians, etc., is worthy of his notice, and may be useful to him in the progress of the expedition.

I heartily wish a happy issue to all your resolves, and am, sir,

Your most obedient servant.

III. TO WILLIAM FAIRFAX.

WINCHESTER, 5 *May*, 1755.

DEAR SIR:

I overtook the general at Frederic Town, in Maryland. Thence we proceeded to this place, where we shall remain till the arrival of the second division of the train, which we hear left Alexandria on Tuesday last. After that, we shall continue our march to Wills Creek; from whence, it is imagined, we shall not stir till the latter end of this month, for want of wagons and other conveniences of transport over the mountains.

You will naturally conclude, that to pass through Maryland, when no object required it, was an uncommon and an extraordinary route for the general and for Colonel Dunbar's regiment to this place. The reason, however, was obvious. Those who promoted it had rather the communication should be opened that way than through Virginia; but I believe the eyes of the general are now opened, and the imposition detected; consequently, the like will not happen again. I am, etc.

IV. TO JOHN A. WASHINGTON.

FORT CUMBERLAND, 14 *May*, 1755.

DEAR BROTHER:

As wearing boots is quite the mode, and mine are in a declining state, I must beg the favor of you to procure me a pair that are good and neat, and send them to Major Carlyle, who, I hope, will contrive to forward them as quickly as my necessity requires.

I see no prospect of moving from this place soon, as we have neither horses nor wagons enough, and no forage, except what is expected from Philadelphia; therefore, I am well convinced that the trouble and difficulty we must encounter in passing the mountains, for the want of proper conveniences, will equal all the difficulties of the campaign; for I conceive the march of such a train of artillery, in these roads, to be a tremendous undertaking. As to any danger from the enemy, I look upon it as trifling, for I believe the

French will be obliged to exert their utmost force to repel the attacks to the northward, where Governor Shirley and others, with a body of eight thousand men, will annoy their settlements, and attempt their forts.

The general has appointed me one of his aids-de camp, in which character I shall serve this campaign agreeably enough, as I am thereby freed from all commands but his, and give his orders, which must be implicitly obeyed.

I have now a good opportunity, and shall not neglect it, of forming an acquaintance, which may be serviceable hereafter, if I find it worth while to push my fortune in the military line.

I have written to my two female correspondents by this opportunity, one of whose letters I have enclosed to you, and beg your deliverance of it. I shall expect a particular account of all that has happened since my departure.

I am, dear Jack, Your most affectionate brother.

V. TO JOHN A. WASHINGTON.

YOUGHIOGANY, 28 *June*, 1755.

DEAR BROTHER:

Immediately upon our leaving the camp at George's Creek, on the 14th instant, from whence I wrote to you, I was seized with a violent fever and pain of the head, which continued without intermission until the 23d, when I was relieved, by the general's absolutely ordering the physician to give me Dr. James's powders, one of the most excellent medicines in the world. It gave me immediate ease, and removed my fever and other complaints in four days' time. My illness was too violent to suffer me to ride; therefore I was indebted to a covered wagon for some part of my transportation; but even in this I could not continue far. The jolting was so great, that I was left upon the road, with a guard and some necessaries, to wait the arrival of Colonel Dunbar's detachment, which was two days' march behind us, the general giving me his word of honor that I should be brought up before he reached the French fort. This promise, and the doctor's declaration, that if I persevered in my attempts to go on, in the condition I then was, my life would be endangered, determined me to halt for the above mentioned detachment.

As the communication between this and Wills Creek must soon be too dangerous for single persons to pass, it will render the intercourse of letters slow and precarious; therefore I shall attempt (and will go through it if I have strength) to give you an account of our proceedings, our situation, and prospects at present; which I desire you will communicate to Colonel Fairfax, and others, my correspondents, for I am too weak to write more than this letter.

In the letter which I wrote to you from George's Creek, I acquainted you that, unless the number of wagons was retrenched and the carriage-horses increased, we should never be able to see Fort Duquesne. This, in two days afterwards (which was about the time they got to the Little Meadows, with some of their foremost wagons and strongest teams), they themselves were convinced of; for they found that, besides the extreme difficulty of getting the wagons along at all, they had often a line of three or four miles in length; and the soldiers guarding them were so dispersed, that, if we had been attacked either in front, centre, or rear, the part so attacked must have been cut off or totally routed, before they could be sustained by any other corps.

At the Little Meadows a second council was called (for there had been one before), wherein the urgency for horses was again represented to the officers of the different corps, and how laudable a farther retrenchment of their baggage would be, that the spare ones might be turned over for the public service. In order to encourage this, I gave up my best horse, which I have never heard of since, and took no more baggage than half my portmanteau would easily contain. It is said, however, that the number reduced by this second attempt was only from two hundred and ten or twelve, to two hundred, which had no perceivable effect.

The general, before they met in council, asked my private opinion concerning the expedition. I urged him, in the warmest terms I was able, to push forward, if he even did it with a small but chosen band, with such artillery and light stores as were necessary; leaving the heavy artillery, baggage, and the like with the rear division of the army, to follow by slow and easy marches, which they might do safely while we were advanced in front. As one reason to support this opinion, I urged that, if we could credit our intelligence, the French were weak at the Fork at present, but hourly expected reinforcements, which, to my certain knowledge, could not arrive with provisions, or any supplies, during the continuance of the drought, as the Buffalo River (Rivière aux Bœufs), down which was their only communication to Venango, must be as dry as we now found the Great Crossing of the Youghiogany, which may be passed dry-shod.

This advice prevailed, and it was determined that

the general, with one thousand two hundred chosen men, and officers from all the different corps, under the following field officers, viz., Sir Peter Halket, who acts as brigadier, Lieutenant-Colonel Gage, Lieutenant-Colonel Burton, and Major Sparks, with such a number of wagons as the train would absolutely require, should march as soon as things could be got in readiness. This was completed, and we were on our march by the 19th, leaving Colonel Dunbar and Major Chapman behind, with the residue of the two regiments, some independent companies, most of the women, and, in short, everything not absolutely essential, carrying our provisions and other necessaries upon horses.

We set out with less than thirty carriages, including those that transported the ammunition for the howitzers, twelve-pounders, and six-pounders, and all of them strongly horsed; which was a prospect that conveyed infinite delight to my mind, though I was excessively ill at the time. But this prospect was soon clouded, and my hopes brought very low indeed, when I found that, instead of pushing on with vigor, without regarding a little rough road, they were halting to level every mole-hill, and to erect bridges over every brook, by which means we were four days in getting twelve miles.

At this camp I was left by the doctor's advice and the general's positive orders, as I have already mentioned, without which I should not have been prevailed upon to remain behind; as I then imagined, and now believe, I shall find it no easy matter to join my own corps again, which is twenty-five miles in advance. Notwithstanding, I had the general's word of honor, pledged in the most solemn manner, that I should be brought up before he arrived at Fort Duquesne. They have had frequent alarms, and several men have been scalped; but this is done with no other design than to retard the march, and to harass the men, who, if they are to be turned out every time a small party attacks the guards at night (for I am certain they have not sufficient force to make a serious assault), the enemy's aim will be accomplished by the gaining of time.

I have been now six days with Colonel Dunbar's corps, who are in a miserable condition for want of horses, not having enough for their wagons; so that the only method he has of proceeding is to march with as many wagons as these will draw, and then halt till the remainder are brought up with the same horses, which requires two days more; and shortly, I believe, he will not be able to stir at all. There has been vile management in regard to horses.

My strength will not admit of my saying more, though I have not said half that I intended concerning affairs here. Business I shall not think of, but depend solely upon your management of all my affairs, not doubting that they will be well conducted. I am, etc.

VI. TO MRS. MARY WASHINGTON, NEAR FREDERICKSBURG.

FORT CUMBERLAND, 18 *July*, 1755.

HONORED MADAM:

As I doubt not but you have heard of our defeat, and, perhaps, had it represented in a worse light, if possible, than it deserves, I have taken this earliest opportunity to give you some account of the engagement as it happened, within ten miles of the French fort, on Wednesday the 9th instant.

We marched to that place without any considerable loss, having only now and then a straggler picked up by the French and scouting Indians. When we came there we were attacked by a party of French and Indians, whose number, I am persuaded, did not exceed three hundred men; while ours consisted of about one thousand three hundred well-armed troops, chiefly regular soldiers, who were struck with such a panic that they behaved with more cowardice than it is possible to conceive. The officers behaved gallantly in order to encourage their men, for which they suffered greatly, there being near sixty killed and wounded; a large proportion of the number we had.

The Virginia troops showed a good deal of bravery, and were nearly all killed; for I believe, out of three companies that were there, scarcely thirty men are left alive. Captain Peyrouny, and all his officers down to a corporal, were killed. Captain Polson had nearly as hard a fate, for only one of his was left. In short, the dastardly behavior of those they call regulars exposed all others, that were inclined to do their duty, to almost certain death; and at last, despite of all the efforts of the officers to the contrary, they ran, as sheep pursued by dogs, and it was impossible to rally them.

The general was wounded, of which he died three days after. Sir Peter Halket was killed in the field, where died many other brave officers. I luckily escaped without a wound, though I had four bullets through my coat, and two horses shot under me. Captains Orme and Morris, two of the aids-de-camp, were wounded early in the engagement, which rendered the duty harder upon me, as I was the only person then left to distribute the general's orders, which I was scarcely able to do, as I was not half recovered from a violent illness that had confined me to my bed and a wagon for above ten days. I am still in a weak and feeble condition, which induces me to halt here two or three days in the hope of recovering a little strength, to enable me to proceed homewards; from whence, I fear, I shall not be able to stir till towards September; so that I shall not have the pleasure of seeing you till then, unless it be in Fairfax. Please to give my love to Mr. Lewis and my sister; and compliments to Mr. Jackson, and all other friends that inquire after me. I am, honored madam, your most dutiful son.

IV.

A VIRGINIA PLANTER.

THE period between the final victory of England over France and the war for the independence of the colonies was one of perplexity and discussion. It is difficult for us to-day to put ourselves in the place of Washington and other men of his time. Washington was a Virginian, and was one of the legislature. He was used to making laws and providing for the needs of the people of Virginia, but he was accustomed to look beyond Virginia to England. There the king was, and he was one of the subjects of the king. Though he and others might never have seen England, it was the centre of the world to them. He thought of the other colonies not so much as all parts of one great country on this side of the Atlantic, as each separately a part of the British empire.

After all, however, and most of all, he was a Virginian. In Virginia he owned land. There was his home, and there his occupation. He was a farmer, a planter of tobacco and wheat; and it was his business to sell his products. As for the French, they were the enemies of Great Britain, but they were also very near enemies of Virginia. They were getting possession of land in Virginia itself, — land which Washington owned in part ; and when he was busily engaged in driving them out, he did not have to stop to think of France ; he needed only to think of Fort Duquesne, a few days' march to the westward.

When, therefore, he found the British government making laws which required him to pay roundly for sending his tobacco to market, and taxing him as if there were no Virginia legislature to say what taxes the people could and should pay, he began to be dissatisfied. England was a great way off ; Virginia was close at hand. He was loyal to the king and had fought under the king's officers, but if the king cared nothing for his loyalty, and only wanted his pence, his loyalty was likely to cool.

Washington had grown up with an intense love of law, and in this he was like other American Englishmen. In England there were very few persons who made the laws. The vast majority had nothing to do but to obey the laws. Yet it is among the makers of laws that the love of law prevails ; and since in America a great many more Englishmen had to do with government in colony and in town than in England, there were more who passionately insisted upon the law being observed. An unlawful act was to them an outrage. When they said that England was oppressing them and making them slaves, they did not mean that they wanted liberty to do what they pleased, but that they wanted to be governed by just laws, made by the men who had the right to make laws. That right belonged to the legislatures, to which they sent representatives.

So it was out of his love of law and justice that Washington and others protested against the Stamp Act ; and when the act was repealed, they threw up their hats and hurrahed, not because they should not have to buy and use stamps, but because by repealing the act, Parliament had as much as said that it was an unlawful act. The two letters which follow, written to Bryan Fairfax, who was a Virginian Englishman disposed to side with Parliament, show how Washington felt and reasoned.

I.

Mount Vernon, 20 *July*, 1774.

Dear Sir:

Your letter of the 17th was not presented to me till after the resolutions, which were judged advisable for this country to adopt, had been revised, altered, and corrected in the committee; nor till we had gone into a general meeting in the court-house, and my attention was necessarily called every moment to the business before us. I did, however, upon the receipt of it, in that hurry and bustle, hastily run it over, and I handed it round to the gentlemen on the bench, of whom there were many; but, as no person present seemed in the least disposed to adopt your sentiments, as there appeared a perfect satisfaction and acquiescence in the measures proposed (except from Mr. Williamson, who was for adopting your advice literally, without obtaining a second voice on his side), and as a gentleman, to whom the letter was shown, advised me not to have it read, as it was not likely to make a convert, and was repugnant, some of them thought, to every principle we were contending for, I forbore to offer it otherwise than in the manner above mentioned; which I shall be sorry for, if it gives you any dissatisfaction that your sentiments were not read to the county at large, instead of being communicated to the first people in it, by offering them the letter in the manner I did.

That I differ very widely from you, in respect to the mode of obtaining a repeal of the acts so much and so justly complained of, I shall not hesitate to acknowledge; and that this difference in opinion probably proceeds from the different constructions we put upon the conduct and intention of the ministry may also be true; but as I see nothing, on the one hand, to induce a belief that the Parliament would embrace a favorable opportunity of repealing acts which they go on with great rapidity to pass in order to enforce their tyrannical system; and, on the other, I observe, or think I observe, that government is pursuing a regular plan at the expense of law and justice to overthrow our constitutional rights and liberties, how can I expect any redress from a measure which has been ineffectually tried already? For, sir, what is it we are contending against? Is it against paying the duty of three pence per pound on tea because burdensome? No; it is the right only, that we have all long disputed; and to this end we have already petitioned his Majesty in as humble and dutiful a manner as subjects could do. Nay, more, we applied to the House of Lords and House of Commons in their different legislative capacities, setting forth, that, as Englishmen, we could not be deprived of this essential and valuable part of our constitution. If, then, as the fact really is, it is against the right of taxation that we now do, and, as I before said, all along have contended, why should they suppose an exertion of this power would be less obnoxious now than formerly? And what reason have we to believe that they would make a second attempt, whilst the same sentiments fill the breast of every American, if they did not intend to enforce it if possible?

The conduct of the Boston people could not justify the rigor of their measures, unless there had been a requisition of payment and refusal of it; nor did that conduct require an act to deprive the government of Massachusetts Bay of their charter, or to exempt offenders from trial in the places where offences were committed, as there was not, nor could there be, a single instance produced to manifest the necessity of it. Are not all these things evident proofs of a fixed and uniform plan to tax us? If we want further proofs, do not all the debates in the House of Commons serve to confirm this? And has not General Gage's conduct since his arrival, in stopping the address of his council and publishing a proclamation more becoming a Turkish bashaw than an English governor, declaring it treason to associate in any manner by which the commerce of Great Britain is to be affected, — has not this exhibited an unexampled testimony of the most despotic system of tyranny that ever was practised in a free government? In short, what further proofs are wanting to satisfy any one of the designs of the ministry than their own acts, which are uniform and plainly tending to the same point, nay, if I mistake not, avowedly to fix the right of taxation? What hope have we then from petitioning, when they tell us that now or never is the time to fix the matter? Shall we, after this, whine and cry for relief, when we have already tried it in vain? Or shall we supinely sit and see one province after another fall a sacrifice to despotism?

If I were in any doubt as to the right which the Parliament of Great Britain had to tax us without our consent, I should most heartily coincide with you in opinion, that to petition, and petition only, is the proper method to apply for relief; because we should then be asking a favor, and not claiming a right, which, by the law of nature and by our constitution, we are, in my opinion, indubitably entitled to. I should even think it criminal to go further than this, under such an idea; but I have none such. I think the Parliament of Great Britain have no more right to put their hands into my pocket, without my consent, than I have to put my hands into yours; and this being already urged to them in a firm but decent manner, by all the colonies, what reason is there to expect anything from their justice?

As to the resolution for addressing the throne, I own to you, sir, I think the whole might as well have been expunged. I expect nothing from the measure, nor should my voice have sanctioned it, if the non-importation scheme was intended to be retarded by it; for I am convinced, as much as I am of my existence, that there is no relief for us but in their distress; and I think, at least I hope, that there is public virtue enough left among us to deny ourselves everything but the bare necessaries of life to accomplish this end. This we have a right to do, and no power upon earth can compel us to do otherwise, till it has first reduced us to the most abject state of slavery. The stopping of our exports would, no doubt, be a shorter method than the other to effect this purpose; but if we owe money to Great Britain, nothing but the last necessity can justify the non-payment of it; and, therefore, I have great doubts upon this head, and wish to see the other method first tried, which is legal and will facilitate these payments.

I cannot conclude without expressing some concern that I should differ so widely in sentiments from you on a matter of such great moment and general import; and I should much distrust my own judgment upon the occasion, if my nature did not recoil at the thought of submitting to measures which I think subversive of everything that I ought to hold dear and valuable, and did I not find, at the same time, that the voice of mankind is with me. I must apologize for sending you so rough a sketch of my thoughts upon your letter. When I look back and see the length of my own, I cannot, as I am a good deal hurried at this time, think of taking off a fair copy.

I am, dear sir, your most obedient humble servant.

II.

MOUNT VERNON, 24 *August*, 1774.

DEAR SIR:

Your letter of the 5th instant came to this place, forwarded by Mr. Ramsay, a few days after my return from Williamsburg, and I delayed acknowledging it sooner, in the hope that I should find time, before I began my journey to Philadelphia, to answer it fully, if not satisfactorily; but, as much of my time has been engrossed since I came home by company, by your brother's sale and the business consequent thereupon, in writing letters to England, and now in attending to my own domestic affairs previous to my departure, I find it impossible to bestow as much attention on the subject of your letter as I could wish, and, therefore, I must rely upon your good nature and candor in excuse for not attempting it. In truth, persuaded as I am that you have read all the political pieces which compose a large share of the gazettes at this time, I should think it, but for your request, a piece of inexcusable arrogance in me to make the least essay towards a change in your political opinions; for I am sure I have no new light to throw upon the subject, nor any other arguments to offer in support of my own doctrine, than what you have seen; and I could only in general add, that an innate spirit of freedom first told me that the measures which the administrations have for some time been and now are most violently pursuing, are opposed to every principle of natural justice; whilst much abler heads than my own have fully convinced me, that they are not only repugnant to natural right, but subversive of the laws and constitution of Great Britain itself, in the establishment of which some of the best blood in the kingdom has been spilt.

Satisfied, then, that the acts of the British Parliament are no longer governed by the principles of justice, that they are trampling upon the valuable rights of Americans, confirmed to them by charter and by the constitution they themselves boast of, and convinced beyond the smallest doubt that these measures are the result of deliberation, and attempted to be carried into execution by the hand of power, is it a time to trifle, or risk our cause upon petitions, which with difficulty obtain access, and afterwards are thrown by with the utmost contempt? Or should we, because heretofore unsuspicious of design, and then unwilling to enter into disputes with the mother country, go on to bear more, and forbear to enumerate our just causes of complaint? For my own part, I shall not undertake to say where the line between Great Britain and the colonies should be drawn; but I am clearly of opinion that one ought to be drawn, and our rights clearly ascertained. I could wish, I own, that the dispute had been left to posterity to determine, but the crisis is arrived when we must assert our rights, or submit to every imposition, that can be heaped upon us, till custom and use shall make us tame and abject slaves.

I intended to write no more than an apology for not writing; but I find I am insensibly running into a length I did not expect, and therefore shall conclude with remarking, that, if you disavow the right of Parliament to tax us, unrepresented as we are, we only differ in respect to the mode of opposition, and this difference principally arises from your belief, that they (the Parliament, I mean,) want a decent opportunity to repeal the acts; whilst I am fully convinced that there has been a regular, systematic plan formed to enforce them, and that nothing but unanimity and firmness in the colonies, which they did not expect, can prevent it. By the best advices from Boston it seems that General Gage is exceedingly disconcerted at the quiet and steady conduct of the people of the Massachusetts Bay, and at the measures pursuing by the other governments. I dare say he expected to force those oppressed people into compliance, or irritate them to acts of violence before this, for a more colorable pretence of ruling that and the other colonies with a high hand.

I shall set off on Wednesday next for Philadelphia, where, if you have any commands, I shall be glad to oblige you in them; being, dear sir, with real regard.

Your most obedient servant.

V.

COMMANDER-IN-CHIEF.

When the second Continental Congress met in May, 1775, Washington was a delegate from Virginia. Every one felt the gravity and delicacy of the situation. An army had been raised, but it was a New England army, for it had been started into life by the fight at Lexington and Concord. If the coming struggle was to be at Boston, as seemed likely, it was natural that the troops should come mainly from that neighborhood. The colonies were widely separated; they had not acted much together, would it not be better, would it not save ill-feeling, if a New England man were to command this New England army?

There were some who thought thus; and besides, there was still a good deal of difference of opinion as to the course to be pursued. Some were ready for independence; others, and perhaps the most, hoped to bring the British to terms. Parties were rising in Congress; petty jealousies were showing themselves, when suddenly John Adams of Massachusetts, seeing into what perplexities they were drifting, came forward with a distinct proposition that Congress should adopt the army before Boston and appoint a commander. He did not name Washington, but described him as a certain gentleman from Virginia who could unite the cordial exertions of all the colonies better than any other person. No one doubted who was meant, and Washington, confused and agitated, left the room at once.

Nothing else was talked of. The delegates discussed the matter in groups and small circles, and a few days afterward a Maryland delegate formally nominated George Washington to be commander-in-chief of the American Army. He was unanimously elected, but the honor of bringing him distinctly before the Congress belongs to John Adams. It seems now a very natural thing to do, but really it was something which required wisdom and courage. When one sums up all Washington's military experience at this time, it was not great, or such as to point him out as unmistakably the leader of the American army. There was a general then in command at Cambridge, who had seen more of war than Washington had. But Washington was the leading military man in Virginia, and it was for this reason that John Adams as a New England man urged his election. The Congress had done something to bring the colonies together; the war was to do more, but probably no single act had a more far-reaching significance in making the Union, than the act of naming for the chief place the Virginia Washington by the New England Adams.

It was on the 15th day of June, 1775, that George Washington was chosen commander-in-chief. The next day he made his answer to Congress, in which he declared that he accepted the office, but that he would take no pay; he would keep an exact account of his expenses, but he would give his services to his country. There was no time to be lost. He could not go home to bid his wife good-by, and he did not know when he should see her again, so he wrote her from Philadelphia. He had left a relation, Mr. Lund Washington, in charge of the Mount Vernon estate, and later in the year he wrote to him a letter of instructions about the care of his place. The three letters follow.

I. TO THE PRESIDENT OF CONGRESS.

Mr. President: Though I am truly sensible of the high honor done me, in this appointment, yet I feel great distress, from a consciousness that my abilities and military experience may not be equal to the extensive and important trust. However, as the Congress desire it, I will enter upon the momentous duty, and exert every power I possess in their service, and for the support of the glorious cause. I beg they will accept my most cordial thanks for this distinguished testimony of their approbation.

But, lest some unlucky event should happen, unfavorable to my reputation, I beg it may be remembered by every gentleman in the room, that I, this day, declare with the utmost sincerity, I do not think myself equal to the command I am honored with.

As to pay, sir. I beg leave to assure the Congress, that, as no pecuniary consideration could have tempted me to accept this arduous employment at the expense of my domestic ease and happiness, I do not wish to make any profit from it. I will keep an exact account of my expenses. Those, I doubt not, they will discharge; and that is all I desire.

II. TO MRS. MARTHA WASHINGTON.

My Dearest: I am now set down to write tc you on a subject which fills me with inexpressible concern, and this concern is greatly aggravated and increased when I reflect upon the uneasiness I know it will give you. It has been determined in Congress, that the whole army raised for the defence of the American cause shall be put under my care, and that it is necessary for me to proceed immediately to Boston to take upon me the command of it.

You may believe me, my dear Patsy, when I assure you in the most solemn manner, that, so far from seeking this appointment, I have used every endeavor in my power to avoid it, not only from my unwillingness to part with you and the family, but from a consciousness of its being a trust too great for my capacity, and that I should enjoy more real happiness in one month with you at home, than I have the most distant prospect of finding abroad, if my stay were to be seven times seven years. But as it has been a kind of destiny that has thrown me upon this service, I shall hope that my undertaking it is designed to answer some good purpose. You might, and I suppose did perceive, from the tenor of my letters, that I was apprehensive I could not avoid this appointment, as I did not pretend to intimate when I should return. That was the case. It was utterly out of my power to refuse this appointment without exposing my character to such censures as would have reflected dishonor upon myself, and given pain to my friends. This, I am sure, could not, and ought not, to be pleasing to you, and must have lessened me considerably in my own esteem. I shall rely, therefore, confidently on that Providence which has heretofore preserved and been bountiful to me, not doubting but that I shall return safe to you in the fall. I shall feel no pain from the toil or the danger of the campaign; my unhappiness will flow from the uneasiness I know you will feel from being left alone. I therefore beg that you will summon your whole fortitude, and pass your time as agreeably as possible. Nothing will give me so much sincere satisfaction as to hear this, and to hear it from your own pen. My earnest and ardent desire is, that you would pursue any plan that is most likely to produce content and a tolerable degree of tranquillity; as it must add greatly to my uneasy feelings to hear that you are dissatisfied or complaining at what I really could not avoid.

As life is always uncertain, and common prudence dictates to every man the necessity of settling his temporal concerns while it is in his power, and while the mind is calm and undisturbed, I have, since I came to this place (for I had not time to do it before I left home), got Colonel Pendleton to draft a will for me, by the directions I gave him, which I will now enclose. The provision made for you in case of my death, will, I hope, be agreeable.

I shall add nothing more, as I have several letters to write, but to desire that you will remember me to your friends, and to assure you that I am, with the most unfeigned regard, my dear Patsy, your affectionate, &c.

III. TO LUND WASHINGTON.

I well know where the difficulty of accomplishing these things will lie. Overseers are already engaged, upon shares, to look after my business. Remote advantages to me, however manifest and beneficial, are nothing to them; and to engage standing wages, when I do not know that anything that I have or can raise will command cash, is attended with hazard; for which reason I hardly know what more to say than to discover to you my wishes. The same reason, although it may in appearance have the same tendency in respect to you, shall not be the same in its operation; for I will engage for the year coming, and the year following, if these troubles and my absence continue, that your wages shall be standing and certain, at the highest amount, that any one year's crop has produced to you yet. I do not offer this as any temptation to induce you to go on more cheerfully in prosecuting these schemes of mine. I should do injustice to you, were I not to acknowledge that your conduct has ever appeared to me above everything sordid; but I offer it in consideration of the great charge you have upon your hands, and my entire dependence upon your fidelity and industry.

It is the greatest, indeed it is the only comfortable reflection I enjoy on this score, that my business is in the hands of a person concerning whose integrity I have not a doubt, and on whose care I can rely. Were it not for this, I should feel very unhappy on account of the situation of my affairs; but I am persuaded you will do for me as you would for yourself, and more than this I cannot expect.

Let the hospitality of the house with respect to the poor be kept up. Let no one go hungry away. If any of this kind of people should be in want of corn, supply their necessities, provided it does not encourage them in idleness; and I have no objection to your giving my money in charity, to the amount of forty or fifty pounds a year, when you think it well bestowed. What I mean by having no objection is, that it is my desire that it should be done. You are to consider, that neither myself nor wife is now in the way to do these good offices. In all other respects I recommend it to you, and have no doubt of your observing the greatest economy and frugality; as I suppose you know that I do not get a farthing for my services here, more than my expenses. It becomes necessary, therefore, for me to be saving at home

VI.

IN CAMP AT CAMBRIDGE.

On the 2d day of July, 1775, Washington arrived at Cambridge where the little army which he was to command was gathered. The next day, with Lee and other officers he rode to the Common, and there, under an elm-tree still standing, took command of the American army. The men were in companies of various sizes, under captains and other officers who had very little authority over the privates, who usually elected their own commander. A visitor to the camp relates a dialogue which he heard between a captain and one of the privates under him.

"Bill," said the captain, "go and bring a pail of water for the men."

"I shan't," said Bill. "It 's your turn now, captain; I got it last time."

But the men, though under very little discipline, were good stuff out of which to make soldiers. Most of them were in dead earnest, and they brought, besides courage, great skill in the use of the ordinary musket. A story is told of a company of riflemen raised in one of the frontier counties of Pennsylvania. So many volunteers applied as to embarrass the leader who was enlisting the company, and he drew on a board with chalk the figure of a nose of the common size, placed the board at a distance of a hundred and fifty yards, and then declared he would take only those who could hit the mark. Over sixty succeeded. "General Gage, take care of *your* nose," says the newspaper that tells the story. General Gage was at that time the commander of the British forces in Boston.

As soon as he could look about him and see what he had to depend upon, and what he needed, Washington wrote to the President of Congress, and began that series of letters which continued throughout the war. His first letter was written a week after he took command. He wrote also to his familiar friends and family, and a second letter is here given to his brother John. A third letter, written in the winter following to Joseph Reed, shows what difficulty Washington found in carrying on the siege.

I. TO THE PRESIDENT OF CONGRESS.

CAMP AT CAMBRIDGE, 10 *July*, 1775.

SIR: I arrived safe at this place on the 3d instant, after a journey attended with a good deal of fatigue, and retarded by necessary attentions to the successive civilities, which accompanied me in my whole route.

Upon my arrival, I immediately visited the several posts occupied by our troops; and, as soon as the weather permitted, reconnoitred those of the enemy. I found the latter strongly intrenching on Bunker's Hill, about a mile from Charlestown, and advanced about a mile from the place of the late action, with their sentries extended about one hundred and fifty yards on this side of the narrowest part of the neck leading from this place to Charlestown. Three floating batteries lie in Mystic River near their camp, and one twenty-gun ship below the ferry-place between Boston and Charlestown. They have also a battery on Cops Hill, on the Boston side, which much annoyed our troops in the late attack. Upon Roxbury Neck, they are also deeply intrenched and strongly fortified. Their advanced guards, till last Saturday, occupied Brown's houses, about a mile from Roxbury meeting-house, and twenty rods from their lines; but at that time a party from General Thomas's camp surprised the guard, drove them in, and burned the houses. The bulk of their army, commanded by General Howe, lies on Bunker's Hill, and the remainder on Roxbury Neck, except the light-horse and a few men in the town of Boston.

On our side, we have thrown up intrenchments on Winter and Prospect Hills, the enemy's camp in full view, at the distance of little more than a mile. Such intermediate points as would admit a landing, I have since my arrival taken care to strengthen, down to Sewall's farm, where a strong intrenchment has been thrown up. At Roxbury, General Thomas has thrown up a strong work on the hill, about two hundred yards above the meeting-house; which, with the brokenness of the ground, and a great number of rocks, has made that pass very secure. The troops raised in New Hampshire, with a regiment from Rhode Island, occupy Winter Hill; a part of those from Connecticut, under General Putnam, are on Prospect Hill. The troops in this town are entirely of the Massachusetts; the remainder of the Rhode Island men are at Sewall's farm. Two regiments of Connecticut, and nine of the Massachusetts, are at Roxbury. The residue of the army, to the number of about seven hundred, are posted in several small towns along the coast, to prevent the depredations of the enemy.

Upon the whole, I think myself authorized to say, that, considering the great extent of line and the nature of the ground, we are as well secured as could be expected in so short a time, and with the disadvantages we labor under. These consist in a want of engineers to construct proper works and direct the men, a want of tools, and a sufficient number of men to man the works in case of an attack. You will observe, by the proceedings of the council of war, which I have the honor to enclose, that it is our unanimous opinion to hold and defend these works as long as possible. The discouragement it would give the men, and its contrary effects on the ministerial troops, thus to abandon our encampment in their face, formed with so much labor and expense, added to the certain destruction of a considerable and valuable extent of country, and our uncertainty of finding a place in all respects so capable of making a stand, are leading reasons for this determination. At the same time we are very sensible of the difficulties which attend the defence of lines of so great extent, and the dangers which may ensue from such a division of the army.

My earnest wish to comply with the instructions of the Congress, in making an early and complete return of the state of the army, has led to an involuntary delay of addressing you; which has given me much concern. Having given orders for that purpose immediately on my arrival, and not then so well apprised of the imperfect obedience which had been paid to those of the like nature from General Ward, I was led from day to day to expect they would come in, and therefore detained the messenger. They are not now so complete as I could wish; but much allowance is to be made for inexperience in forms, and a liberty which had been taken (not given) on the subject. These reasons, I flatter myself, will no longer exist; and, of consequence, more regularity and exactness will in future prevail. This, with a necessary attention to the lines, the movements of the ministerial troops, and our immediate security, must be my apology, which I beg you to lay before Congress with the utmost duty and respect.

We labor under great disadvantages for want of tents; for, though they have been helped out by a collection of sails from the seaport towns, the number is far short of our necessities. The colleges and houses of this town are necessarily occupied by the troops; which affords another reason for keeping our present station. But I most sincerely wish the whole army was properly provided to take the field, as I am well assured, that, besides greater expedition and activity in case of alarm, it would highly conduce to health and discipline. As materials are not to be had here, I would beg leave to recommend the procuring of a farther supply from Philadelphia as soon as possible.

I should be extremely deficient in gratitude, as well as justice, if I did not take the first opportunity to acknowledge the readiness and attention, which the Provincial Congress[1] and different committees have shown, to make everything as convenient and agreeable as possible. But there is a vital and inherent principle of delay incompatible with military service, in transacting business through such numerous and different channels. I esteem it, therefore, my duty to represent the inconvenience which must unavoidably ensue from a dependence on a number of persons for supplies; and submit it to the consideration of Congress, whether the public service will not be best promoted by appointing a commissary-general for these purposes. We have a striking instance of the preference of such a mode, in the establishment of Connecticut, as their troops are extremely well provided under the direction of Mr. Trumbull, and he has at different times assisted others with various articles. Should my sentiments happily coincide with those of your Honors on this subject, I beg leave to propose Mr. Trumbull as a very proper person for this department. In the arrangement of troops collected under such circumstances, and upon the spur of immediate necessity, several appointments have been omitted, which appear to be indispensably necessary for the good government of the army, particularly a quarter-

[1] That is, the congress formed by the patriots in Massachusetts.

master-general, a commissary of musters, and a commissary of artillery. These I must particularly recommend to the notice and provision of the Congress.

I find myself already much embarrassed for want of a military chest. These embarrassments will increase every day. I must therefore most earnestly request that money may be forwarded as soon as possible. The want of this most necessary article will, I fear, produce great inconveniences, if not prevented by an early attention. I find the army in general, and the troops raised in Massachusetts in particular, very deficient in necessary clothing. Upon inquiry, there appears no probability of obtaining any supplies in this quarter; and, on the best consideration of this matter I am able to form, I am of opinion that a number of hunting-shirts, not less than ten thousand, would in a great degree remove this difficulty, in the cheapest and quickest manner. I know nothing, in a speculative view, more trivial, yet which, if put in practice, would have a happier tendency to unite the men, and abolish those provincial distinctions that lead to jealousy and dissatisfaction.

In a former part of this letter I mentioned the want of engineers. I can hardly express the disappointment I have experienced on this subject, the skill of those we have being very imperfect, and confined to the mere manual exercise of cannon; whereas the war in which we are engaged requires a knowledge, comprehending the duties of the field, and fortification. If any persons thus qualified are to be found in the southern colonies, it would be of great public service to forward them with all expedition.

Upon the article of ammunition I must reëcho the former complaints on this subject. We are so exceedingly destitute, that our artillery will be of little use, without a supply both large and seasonable. What we have must be reserved for the small arms, and that managed with the utmost frugality.

I am very sorry to observe that the appointment of general officers, in the provinces of Massachusetts and Connecticut, has not corresponded with the wishes and judgment of either the civil or military. The great dissatisfaction expressed on this subject, and the apparent danger of throwing the whole army into the utmost disorder, together with the strong representations made by the Provincial Congress, have induced me to retain the commissions in my hands until the pleasure of the Continental Congress should be further known, except General Putnam's, which was given the day I came to the camp, and before I was apprised of these disgusts. In such a step, I must beg the Congress will do me the justice to believe that I have been actuated solely by a regard to the public good.

I have not, nor could I have, any private attachments ; every gentleman in appointment was a stranger to me, but from character ; I must, therefore, rely upon the candor and indulgence of Congress for their most favorable construction of my conduct in this particular. General Spencer's disgust was so great at General Putnam's promotion, that he left the army without visiting me, or making known his intention in any respect.

General Pomroy had also retired before my arrival, occasioned, as it is said, by some disappointment from the Provincial Congress. General Thomas is much esteemed, and most earnestly desired to continue in the service ; and, as far as my opportunities have enabled me to judge, I must join in the general opinion, that he is an able, good officer; and his resignation would be a public loss. The postponing of him to Pomroy and Heath, whom he has commanded, would make his continuance very difficult, and probably operate on his mind, as the like circumstances did on that of Spencer.

The state of the army you will find ascertained with tolerable precision in the returns which accompany this letter. Upon finding the number of men to fall so far short of the establishment, and below all expectation, I immediately called a council of the general officers, whose opinion as to the mode of filling up the regiments, and providing for the present exigency, I have the honor of enclosing, together with the best judgment we are able to form of the ministerial troops. From the number of boys, deserters, and negroes, that have been enlisted in the troops of this province, I entertain some doubts whether the number required can be raised here; and all the general officers agree that no dependence can be put on the militia for a continuance in camp, or regularity and discipline during the short time they may stay. This unhappy and devoted province has been so long in a state of anarchy, and the yoke of ministerial oppression has been laid so heavily on it, that great allowances are to be made for troops raised under such circumstances. The deficiency of numbers, discipline, and stores, can only lead to this conclusion, that their spirit has exceeded their strength. But, at the same time, I would humbly submit to the consideration of Congress the propriety of making some further provision of men from the other colonies. If these regiments should be completed to their establishment, the dismission of those unfit for duty, on account of their age and character, would occasion a considerable reduction; and, at all events, they have been enlisted upon such terms that they may be disbanded when other troops arrive. But should my apprehensions be realized, and the regiments here not be filled up, the public cause would suffer by an absolute dependence upon so doubtful an event, unless some provision is made against such a disappointment.

It requires no military skill to judge of the difficulty of introducing proper discipline and subordination into an army, while we have the enemy in view, and are in daily expectation of an attack; but it is of so much importance that every effort will be made to this end which time and circumstances will admit. In the mean time, I have a sincere pleasure in observing, that there are materials for a good army, a great number of able-bodied men, active, zealous in the cause, and of unquestionable courage.

I am now, sir, to acknowledge the receipt of your favor of the 28th of June, enclosing the resolutions of Congress of the 27th, and a copy of a letter from the Committee of Albany; to all which I shall pay due attention.

Generals Gates and Sullivan have both arrived in good health.

My best abilities are at all times devoted to the service of my country; but I feel the weight, importance, and variety of my present duties too sensibly, not to wish a more immediate and frequent communication with the Congress. I fear it may often happen, in the course of our present operations, that I shall need that assistance and direction from them, which time and distance will not allow me to receive.

Since writing the above, I have also to acknowledge

your favor of the 4th instant by Fessenden, and the receipt of the commissions and articles of war. Among the other returns, I have also sent one of our killed, wounded, and missing, in the late action; but have been able to procure no certain account of the loss of the ministerial troops. My best intelligence fixes it at about five hundred killed and six or seven hundred wounded; but it is no more than conjecture, the utmost pains being taken on their side to conceal their loss.

Having ordered the commanding officer to give me the earliest intelligence of every motion of the enemy by land or water, discernible from the heights of his camp, I this instant, as I was closing my letter, received the enclosed from the brigade-major. The design of this manœuvre I know not; perhaps it may be to make a descent somewhere along the coast; it may be for New York; or it may be practised as a deception on us. I thought it not improper, however, to mention the matter to you; I have done the same to the commanding officer at New York; and I shall let it be known to the Committee of Safety here, so that intelligence may be communicated, as they shall think best, along the sea-coast of this government.

I have the honor to be, etc.

II. TO JOHN AUGUSTINE WASHINGTON.

CAMP AT WASHINGTON, 27 *July*, 1775.

DEAR BROTHER: On the 2d instant I arrived at this place, after passing through a great deal of delightful country, covered with grass (although the season has been dry), in a manner very different from our lands in Virginia.

I found a mixed multitude of people here, under very little discipline, order, or government; the enemy in possession of a place called Bunker's Hill on Charlestown Neck, strongly intrenched, and fortifying themselves; part of our own army on two hills, called Winter and Prospect Hills, about a mile and a quarter from the enemy on Bunker's Hill, in a very insecure state; another part at this village; and a third part at Roxbury, guarding the entrance in and out of Boston. My whole time, since I came here, has been employed in throwing up lines of defence at these three several places, to secure, in the first instance, our own troops from any attempts of the enemy; and, in the next place, to cut off all communication between their troops and the country. To do this, and to prevent them from penetrating into the country with fire and sword, and to harass them if they do, is all that is expected of me. If effected, it must totally overthrow the designs of administration, as the whole force of Great Britain in the town and harbor of Boston can answer no other end than to sink her under the disgrace and weight of the expense. The enemy's strength, including marine forces, is computed, from the best accounts I can get, at about twelve thousand men; ours, including sick and absent, at about sixteen thousand; but then we have to guard a semicircle of eight or nine miles, to every part of which we are obliged to be equally attentive; whilst they, situated as it were in the centre of the semicircle, and having the entire command of the water, can bend their whole force against any one part of it with equal facility. This renders our situation not very agreeable, though necessary. However, by incessant labor, Sundays not excepted, we are in a much better posture of defence now than when I first came. The enclosed, though rough, will give you some small idea of Boston and the Bay on this side, as also of the post they have taken on Charlestown Neck at Bunker's Hill, and of our posts.

The enemy are sickly and in want of fresh provisions. Beef, which is chiefly got by slaughtering their milch cows in Boston, sells from one shilling to eighteen pence sterling per pound; and that it may not become cheaper or more plenty, I have driven all the stock within a considerable distance of this place back into the country, out of the way of the men-of-war's boats. In short, I have done, and shall continue to do, everything in my power to distress them. The transports have all arrived, and their whole reinforcement is landed, so that I can see no reason why they should not, if they ever attempt it, come boldly out, and put the matter to issue at once. If they think themselves not strong enough to do this, they surely will carry their arms (having ships of war and transports ready) to some other part of the continent, or relinquish the dispute; the last of which the ministry, unless compelled, will never agree to do. Our works and those of the enemy are so near, and the space between is so open, that each sees everything the other is doing.

I recollect nothing more worth mentioning. I shall therefore conclude, with my best wishes and love to my sister and the family, and compliments to any inquiring friends.

Your most affectionate brother.

III. TO JOSEPH REED.

CAMBRIDGE, 14 *January*, 1776.

DEAR SIR: The bearer presents an opportunity to me of acknowledging the receipt of your favor of the 30th ultimo, which never came to my hands till last night, and, if I have not done it before, of your other letter of the 23d preceding.

The hints you have communicated from time to time not only deserve, but do most sincerely and cordially meet with my thanks. You cannot render a more acceptable service, nor in my estimation give me a more convincing proof of your friendship, than by a free, open, and undisguised account of every matter relative to myself or conduct. I can bear to hear of imputed or real errors. The man who wishes to stand well in the opinion of others, must do this; because he is thereby enabled to correct his faults or remove the prejudices which are imbibed against him. For this reason, I shall thank you for giving me the opinions of the world upon such points as you know me to be interested in; for, as I have but one capital object in view, I could wish to make my conduct coincide with the wishes of mankind, as far as I can consistently; I mean, without departing from that great line of duty which, though hid under a cloud for some time, from a peculiarity of circumstances, may nevertheless bear a scrutiny.

My constant attention to the great and perplexing objects, which continually rise to my view, absorbs all lesser considerations, and indeed scarcely allows me to reflect that there is such a body in existence as the General Court of this colony, but when I am reminded of it by a committee; nor can I, upon recollection, discover in what instances (I wish they would be more explicit) I have been inattentive to, or slighted them. They could not, surely, conceive that there was a propriety in unbosoming the secrets of an army to them; that it was necessary to ask their opinion of throwing up an intrenchment, or forming a battalion. It must, therefore, be what I before hinted to you; and how to remedy it I hardly know, as I am acquainted with few of the members, never go out of my own lines, nor see any of them in them.

I am exceedingly sorry to hear that your little fleet has been shut in by the frost. I hope it has sailed ere this, and given you some proof of the utility of it, and enabled the Congress to bestow a little more attention to the affairs of this army, which suffers exceedingly by their overmuch business, or too little attention to it. We are now without any money in our treasury, powder in our magazines, or arms in our stores. We are without a brigadier (the want of whom has been twenty times urged), engineers, expresses (though a committee has been appointed these two months to establish them), and by and by, when we shall be called upon to take the field, shall not have a tent to lie in. Apropos, what is doing with mine?

These are evils, but small in comparison of those which disturb my present repose. Our enlistments are at a stand; the fears I ever entertained are realized; that is, the *discontented officers* (for I do not know how else to account for it) have thrown such difficulties or stumbling-blocks in the way of recruiting, that I no longer entertain a hope of completing the army by voluntary enlistments, and I see no move or likelihood to do it by other means. In the two last weeks we have enlisted but about a thousand men; whereas I was confidently led to believe, by all the officers I conversed with, that we should by this time have had the regiments nearly completed. Our total number upon paper amounts to about ten thousand five hundred; but as a large portion of these are returned *not joined*, I never expect to receive them, as an ineffectual order has once issued to call them in. Another is now gone forth, peremptorily requiring all officers, under pain of being cashiered, and recruits of being treated as deserters, to join their respective regiments by the 1st day of next month, that I may know my real strength; but if my fears are not imaginary, I shall have a dreadful account of the advanced month's pay. In consequence of the assurances given, and my expectation of having at least men enough enlisted to defend our lines, to which may be added my unwillingness to burden the cause with unnecessary expense, no relief of militia has been ordered in to supply the places of those who are released from their engagements to-morrow, and as to whom, though many have promised to continue out the month, there is no security for their stay.

Thus am I situated with respect to men. With regard to arms I am yet worse off. Before the dissolution of the old army, I issued an order directing three judicious men of each brigade to attend, review, and appraise the good arms of every regiment; and finding a very great unwillingness in the men to part with their arms, at the same time not having it in my power to pay them for the months of November and December, I threatened severely, that every soldier, who should carry away his firelock without leave, should never receive pay for those months; yet so many have been carried off, partly by stealth, but chiefly as condemned, that we have not at this time one hundred guns in the stores, of all that have been taken in the prize-ship and from the soldiery, notwithstanding our regiments are not half complete. At the same time I am told, and believe it, that to restrain the enlistment to men with arms, you will get but few of the former, and still fewer of the latter which would be good for anything.

How to get furnished I know not. I have applied to this and the neighboring colonies, but with what success time only can tell. The reflection on my situation, and that of this army, produces many an unhappy hour when all around me are wrapped in sleep. Few people know the predicament we are in, on a thousand accounts; fewer still will believe, if any disaster happens to these lines, from what cause it flows. I have often thought how much happier I should have been, if, instead of accepting the command under such circumstances, I had taken my musket on my shoulder and entered the ranks, or, if I could have justified the measure to posterity and my own conscience, had retired to the back country, and lived in a wigwam. If I shall be able to rise superior to these and many other difficulties which might be enumerated, I shall most religiously believe that the finger of Providence is in it, to blind the eyes of our enemies; for surely if we get well through this month, it must be for want of their knowing the disadvantages we labor under.

Could I have foreseen the difficulties which have come upon us; could I have known that such a backwardness would have been discovered among the old soldiers to the service, all the generals upon earth should not have convinced me of the propriety of delaying an attack upon Boston till this time. When it can now be attempted, I will not undertake to say; but thus much I will answer for, that no opportunity can present itself earlier than my wishes. But as this letter discloses some interesting truths, I shall be somewhat uneasy until I hear it gets to your hands, although the conveyance is thought safe.

VII.

MR. WASHINGTON OR GENERAL WASHINGTON.

Not long after the declaration of independence an English fleet arrived in New York Bay, bringing a large body of troops, under the command of Lord Howe, who with his brother, Admiral Howe, had been appointed commissioners to treat with the Americans. In reality, they only brought a promise of pardon to rebels. It was very clear to Washington that the British government had not the slightest intention of listening to the grievances of the colonies with a desire to redress them ; but that they meant by these proposals to distract the colonies if possible and build up a party among them that would oppose the action of Congress. There was a little incident attending the arrival of the commissioners that showed the feeling which prevailed. The letter which follows, written by Washington to the President of Congress, describes the affair. Possibly it sounds like very small business. In reality it meant a great deal. Were Washington and other officers rebels against the king, or were they the officers of a government which had declared itself independent of the king? Lord Howe gave up trying to force Washington into the trap, and wrote to his government that it would be necessary in future to give the American commander his title. Little things like this went a great way toward making the people stand erect and look the world in the face.

TO THE PRESIDENT OF CONGRESS.

New York, 14 *July*, 1776.

Sir : General Sullivan, in a letter of the 2d instant, informs me of his arrival with the army at Crown Point, where he is fortifying and throwing up works. He adds, that he has secured all the stores except three cannon left at Chamblee, which in part is made up by taking a fine twelve-pounder out of the lake. The army is sickly, many with the small-pox ; and he is apprehensive the militia, ordered to join them, will not escape the infection. An officer, whom he had sent to reconnoitre, had reported that he saw at St. John's about a hundred and fifty tents, twenty at St. Roy's, and fifteen at Chamblee; and works at the first were busily carrying on.

About three o'clock this afternoon I was informed that a flag from Lord Howe was coming up, and waited with two of our whale-boats until directions should be given. I immediately convened such of the general officers as were not upon other duty, who agreed in opinion that I ought not to receive any letter directed to me as a private gentleman; but if otherwise, and the officer desired to come up to deliver the letter himself, as was suggested, he should come under a safe-conduct. Upon this, I directed Colonel Reed to go down and manage the affair under the above general instruction. On his return he informed me, that, after the common civilities, the officer acquainted him that he had a letter from Lord Howe to Mr. Washington, which he showed under a superscription, "To George Washington, Esq." Colonel Reed replied that there was no such person in the army, and that a letter intended for the General could not be received under such a direction. The officer expressed great concern, said it was a letter rather of a civil than military nature, that Lord Howe regretted he had not arrived sooner, that he (Lord Howe) had great powers. The anxiety to have the letter received was very evident, though the officer disclaimed all knowledge of its contents. However, Colonel Reed's instructions being positive, they parted. After they had got some distance, the officer with the flag again put about, and asked under what direction Mr. Washington chose to be addressed: to which Colonel Reed answered that his station was well known, and that certainly they could be at no loss how to direct to him. The officer said they knew and lamented it; and again repeated his wish, that the letter could be received. Colonel Reed told him a proper direction would obviate all difficulties, and that this was no new matter, this subject having been fully discussed in the course of the last year, of which Lord Howe could not be ignorant; upon which they parted.

I would not upon any occasion sacrifice essentials to punctilio; but in this instance, the opinion of others concurring with my own, I deemed it a duty to my country and my appointment to insist upon that respect which, in any other than a public view, I would willingly have waived. Nor do I doubt but, from the supposed nature of the message, and the anxiety expressed, they will either repeat their flag, or fall upon some mode to communicate the import and consequence of it.

The passage of the ships of war and tenders up the river is a matter of great importance, and has excited much conjecture and speculation. To me two things have occurred as leading them to this proceeding: first, a design to seize on the narrow passes on both sides of the river, giving almost the only land communication with Albany, and of consequence with our northern army, for which purpose they might have troops concealed on board, which they deemed competent of themselves, as the defiles are narrow; or that they would be joined by many disaffected persons in that quarter. Others have added a probability of their having a large quantity of arms on board, to be in readiness to put into the hands of the Tories immediately on the arrival of the fleet, or rather at the time they intend to make their attack. The second is, to cut off entirely all intercourse between this place and Albany by water, and the upper country, and to prevent supplies of every kind from going and coming.

These matters are truly alarming, and of such importance, that I have written to the Provincial Congress of New York, and recommended to their serious consideration the adoption of every possible expedient to guard against the two first; and have suggested the propriety of their employing the militia, or some part of them, in the counties in which these defiles are, to keep the enemy from possessing them, till further provision can be made; and to write to the several leading persons on our side in that quarter to be attentive to all the movements of the ships and the disaffected, in order to discover and frustrate whatever pernicious schemes they have in view.

In respect to the second conjecture of my own, and which seems to be generally adopted, I have the pleasure to inform Congress, that, if their design is to keep the armies from provision, the commissary has told me upon inquiry, that he has forwarded supplies to Albany (now there and above it) sufficient for ten thousand men for four months; that he has a sufficiency here for twenty thousand men for three months, and an abundant quantity secured in different parts of the Jerseys for the Flying Camp, besides having about four thousand barrels of flour in some neighboring part of Connecticut. Upon this head, there is but little occasion for any apprehensions, at least for a considerable time.

VIII.

AT VALLEY FORGE.

THE American army was defeated at the battle of Brandywine, September 10, 1777. Afterward, at Germantown, it had better fortune, but the British were in possession of Philadelphia, and Washington led his army into winter-quarters at Valley Forge. The place was equally distant with Philadelphia from the Brandywine and from the ferry across the Delaware into New Jersey. It was too far from Philadelphia to be in peril from attack, and yet it was so near that the American army could, if opportunity offered, descend quickly upon the city. Then it was so protected by hills and streams that the addition of a few lines of fortification made it very secure.

But there was no town at Valley Forge, and it became necessary to provide some shelter for the soldiers other than the canvas tents which served in the field in summer. It was the middle of December when the army began preparations for the winter, and Washington gave directions for the building of the little village. Each hut was to hold twelve persons, and was to be fourteen feet by sixteen, the sides, ends, and roof to be made of logs, and the sides made tight with clay. There was to be a fire-place in the rear of each hut, built of wood, but lined with clay eighteen inches thick. The walls were to be six and a half feet high. Huts were also to be provided for the officers, and to be placed in the rear of those occupied by the troops. All these were to be regularly arranged in streets. A visitor to the camp when the huts were being built wrote of the army: "They appear to me like a family of beavers, every one busy; some carrying logs, others mud, and the rest plastering them together." It was bitter cold, and for a month the men were hard at work.

But in what sort of condition were the men themselves when they began this work? Here is a picture of one of these men on his way to Valley Forge. "His bare feet peep through his worn-out shoes, his legs nearly naked from the tattered remains of an only pair of stockings, his breeches not enough to cover his nakedness, his shirt hanging in strings, his hair disheveled, his face wan and thin, his look hungry, his whole appearance that of a man forsaken and neglected." And the snow was falling! This was one of the privates. The officers were scarcely better off. One was wrapped "in a sort of dressing-gown made from an old blanket or woolen bed-cover." The uniforms were torn and ragged; the guns were rusty; a few only had bayonets; the soldiers carried their powder in tin boxes and cow horns.

To explain why this army was so poor and forlorn, would be to tell a long story. It may be summed up briefly in these words: the army was not taken care of because there was no country to take care of it. There were thirteen States, and each of these States sent troops into the field, but all of the States were jealous of each other. There was a Congress, which undertook to direct the war, but the members of Congress, coming from the several States, were jealous of one another. The first fervor with which they had talked about a common country had died away; there were some very selfish men in Congress, who could not be patriotic enough to think of the whole country.

The truth is, it takes a long time for the people of a country to come to feel that they have a country. Up to the time of the war for independence the people in America did not care much for one another or for America. They had really been preparing to be a nation, but they did not know it. They were angry with Great Britain, and they knew they had been wronged. They were therefore ready to fight; but it does not require so much courage to fight as to endure suffering and to be patient. So it was that the people of America who were most conscious that they were Americans were the men who were in the army, and their wives and mothers and sisters at home. All these were making sacrifices for their country and so learning to love it. The men in the army came from different States, and there was a great deal of State feeling among them; but, after all, they belonged to one army, the continental army, and they had much more in common than they had separately. Especially they had a great leader who made no distinction between Virginians and New England men. Washington felt keenly all the lack of confidence which Congress showed. He saw that the spirit in Congress was one which kept the people divided, while the spirit at Valley Forge kept the people united. It was during this terrible winter that he wrote the following letter.

TO THE PRESIDENT OF CONGRESS.

VALLEY FORGE, 23 *December*, 1777.

SIR: Full as I was in my representation of the matters in the commissary's department yesterday, fresh and more powerful reasons oblige me to add, that I am now convinced beyond a doubt, that, unless some great and capital change suddenly takes place in that line, this army must inevitably be reduced to one or other of these three things: starve, dissolve, or disperse in order to obtain subsistence in the best manner they can. Rest assured, sir, this is not an exaggerated picture, and that I have abundant reason to suppose what I say.

Yesterday afternoon, receiving information that the enemy in force had left the city, and were advancing towards Derby with the apparent design to forage and draw subsistence from that part of the country, I ordered the troops to be in readiness, that I might give every opposition in my power; when behold, to my great mortification, I was not only informed but convinced, that the men were unable to stir on account of provision, and that a dangerous mutiny, begun the night before, and which with difficulty was suppressed by the spirited exertions of some officers, was still much to be apprehended for want of this article. This brought forth the only commissary in the purchasing line in this camp; and, with him, this melancholy and alarming truth, that he had not a single hoof of any kind to slaughter, and not more than twenty-five barrels of flour! From hence form an opinion of our situation when I add that he could not tell when to expect any.

All I could do, under these circumstances, was to

send out a few light parties to watch and harass the enemy, whilst other parties were instantly detached different ways to collect, if possible, as much provision as would satisfy the present pressing wants of the soldiery. But will this answer? No, sir; three or four days of bad weather would prove our destruction. What, then, is to become of the army this winter? And if we are so often without provisions now, what is to become of us in the spring, when our force will be collected, with the aid perhaps of militia to take advantage of an early campaign, before the enemy can be reinforced? These are considerations of great magnitude, meriting the closest attention; and they will, when my own reputation is so intimately connected with the event as to be affected by it, justify my saying, that the present commissaries are by no means equal to the execution of the office, or that the disaffection of the people is past all belief. The misfortune, however, does in my opinion proceed from both causes; and though I have been tender heretofore of giving my opinion, or lodging complaints, as the change in that department took place contrary to my judgment, and the consequences thereof were predicted; yet, finding that the inactivity of the army, whether for want of provisions, clothes, or other essentials, is charged to my account, not only by the common vulgar but by those in power, it is time to speak plain in exculpation of myself. With truth, then, I can declare, that no man in my opinion ever had his measures more impeded than I have, by every department of the army.

Since the month of July we have had no assistance from the quartermaster-general, and to want of assistance from this department the commissary-genera charges great part of his deficiency. To this I am to add, that, notwithstanding it is a standing order, and often repeated, that the troops shall always have two days' provisions by them, that they might be ready at any sudden call; yet an opportunity has scarcely ever offered, of taking advantage of the enemy, that has not been either totally obstructed, or greatly impeded on this account. And this, the great and crying evil, is not all. The soap, vinegar, and other articles allowed by Congress, we see none of, nor have we seen them, I believe, since the Battle of Brandywine. The first, indeed, we have now little occasion for; few men having more than one shirt, many only the moiety of one, and some none at all. In addition to which, as a proof of the little benefit received from a clothier-general, and as a further proof of the inability of an army, under the circumstances of this, to perform the common duties of soldiers, (besides a number of men confined to hospitals for want of shoes, and others in farmers' houses on the same account,) we have, by a field return this day made, no less than two thousand eight hundred and ninety-eight men now in camp unfit for duty, because they are barefoot and otherwise naked. By the same return it appears that our whole strength in Continental troops, including the eastern brigades, which have joined us since the surrender of General Burgoyne, exclusive of the Maryland troops sent to Wilmington, amounts to no more than eight thousand two hundred in camp fit for duty; notwithstanding which, and that since the 4th instant, our numbers fit for duty, from the hardships and exposures they have undergone, particularly on account of blankets (numbers having been obliged, and still are, to sit up all night by fires, instead of taking comfortable rest in a natural and common way), have decreased near two thousand men.

We find gentlemen, without knowing whether the army was really going into winter-quarters or not (for I am sure no resolution of mine would warrant the remonstrance), reprobating the measure as much as if they thought the soldiers were made of stocks or stones, and equally insensible of frost and snow; and moreover, as if they conceived it easily practicable for an inferior army, under the disadvantages I have described ours to be, which are by no means exaggerated, to confine a superior one, in all respects well appointed and provided for a winter's campaign, within the city of Philadelphia, and to cover from depredation and waste the States of Pennsylvania and Jersey. But what makes this matter still more extraordinary in my eye is that these very gentlemen — who were well apprised of the nakedness of the troops from ocular demonstration, who thought their own soldiers worse clad than others, and who advised me near a month ago to postpone the execution of a plan I was about to adopt, in consequence of a resolve of Congress for seizing clothes, under strong assurances that an ample supply would be collected in ten days agreeably to a decree of the State (not one article of which, by the by, is yet come to hand) — should think a winter's campaign, and the covering of these States from the invasion of an enemy, so easy and practicable a business. I can assure those gentlemen, that it is a much easier and less distressing thing to draw remonstrances in a comfortable room by a good fireside, than to occupy a cold bleak hill, and sleep under frost and snow, without clothes or blankets. However, although they seem to have little feeling for the naked and distressed soldiers, I feel superabundantly for them, and from my soul I pity those miseries, which it is neither in my power to relieve nor prevent.

It is for these reasons, therefore, that I have dwelt upon the subject; and it adds not a little to my other difficulties and distress to find that much more is expected of me than is possible to be performed, and that upon the ground of safety and policy I am obliged to conceal the true state of the army from public view, and thereby expose myself to detraction and calumny. The honorable committee of Congress went from camp fully possessed of my sentiments respecting the establishment of this army, the necessity of auditors of accounts, the appointment of officers, and new arrangements. I have no need, therefore, to be prolix upon these subjects, but I refer to the committee. I shall add a word or two to show, first the necessity of some better provision for binding the officers by the tie of interest to the service, as no day nor scarce an hour passes without the offer of a resigned commission; (otherwise I much doubt the practicability of holding the army together much longer, and in this I shall probably be thought the more sincere, when I freely declare that I do not myself expect to derive the smallest benefit from any establishment that Congress may adopt, otherwise than as a member of the community at large in the good, which I am persuaded will result from the measure, by making better officers and better troops;) and, secondly, to point out the necessity of making the appointments and arrangements without loss of time. We have not more than three months in which to prepare a great deal of business. If we let these slip or waste, we shall be labòring under the same difficulties all next campaign, as we have been this, to rectify mistakes and bring things to order.

Military arrangement, and movements in consequence, like the mechanism of a clock, will be imperfect and disordered by the want of a part. In a very sensible degree have I experienced this, in the course of the last summer, several brigades having no brigadiers appointed to them till late, and some not at all; by which means it follows that an additional weight is thrown upon the shoulders of the commander-in-chief, to withdraw his attention from the great line of his duty. The gentlemen of the committee, when they were at camp, talked of an expedient for adjusting these matters, which I highly approved and wish to see adopted: namely, that two or three members of the Board of War, or a committee of Congress, should repair immediately to camp, where the best aid can be had, and with the commanding officer, or a committee of his appointment, prepare and digest the most perfect plan that can be devised for correcting all abuses and making new arrangements; considering what is to be done with the weak and debilitated regiments, if the States to which they belong will not draft men to fill them, for as to enlisting soldiers it seems to me to be totally out of the question; together with many other things that would occur in the course of such a conference; and, after digesting matters in the best manner they can, to submit the whole to the ultimate determination of Congress.

If this measure is approved, I would earnestly advise the immediate execution of it, and that the commissary-general of purchases, whom I rarely see, may be directed to form magazines without a moment's delay in the neighborhood of this camp, in order to secure provision for us in case of bad weather. The quartermaster-general ought also to be busy in his department. In short, there is as much to be done in preparing for a campaign as in the active part of it. Everything depends upon the preparation that is made in the several departments, and the success or misfortunes of the next campaign will more than probably originate with our activity or supineness during this winter.

IX.

FAREWELL TO THE ARMY.

THE terrible winter at Valley Forge was the lowest point of depression reached during the war for independence. The army during that winter was splendidly drilled by Baron Steuben, and in the spring news came that a treaty had been made with France. Cornwallis surrendered October 19, 1781, and after two more years, a treaty of peace was signed with Great Britain, and Washington, November 2, 1783, issued from Princeton, New Jersey, where Congress was in session, the following farewell address.

The United States in Congress assembled, after giving the most honorable testimony to the merits of the federal armies, and presenting them with the thanks of their country for their long, eminent, and faithful services, having thought proper, by their proclamation bearing date the 18th day of October last, to discharge such part of the troops as were engaged for the war, and to permit the officers on furloughs to retire from service, from and after to-morrow; which proclamation having been communicated in the public papers for the information and government of all concerned, it only remains for the commander-in-chief to address himself once more, and that for the last time, to the armies of the United States (however widely dispersed the individuals who composed them may be), and to bid them an affectionate, a long farewell.

But before the commander-in-chief takes his final leave of those he holds most dear, he wishes to indulge himself a few moments in calling to mind a slight review of the past. He will then take the liberty of exploring with his military friends their future prospects, of advising the general line of conduct which, in his opinion, ought to be pursued; and he will conclude the address by expressing the obligations he feels himself under for the spirited and able assistance he has experienced from them, in the performance of an arduous office.

A contemplation of the complete attainment (at a period earlier than could have been expected) of the object for which we contended against so formidable a power, cannot but inspire us with astonishment and gratitude. The disadvantageous circumstances on our part, under which the war was undertaken, can never be forgotten. The singular interpositions of Providence in our feeble condition were such as could scarcely escape the attention of the most unobserving; while the unparalleled perseverance of the armies of the United States, through almost every possible suffering and discouragement for the space of eight long years, was little short of a standing miracle.

It is not the meaning nor within the compass of this address to detail the hardships peculiarly incident to our service, or to describe the distresses which in several instances have resulted from the extremes of hunger and nakedness, combined with the rigors of an inclement season; nor is it necessary to dwell on the dark side of our past affairs. Every American officer and soldier must now console himself for any unpleasant circumstances which may have occurred, by a recollection of the uncommon scenes of which he has been called to act no inglorious part, and the astonishing events of which he has been a witness; events which have seldom, if ever before, taken place on the stage of human action nor can they probably ever happen again. For who has before seen a disciplined army formed at once from such raw materials? Who, that was not a witness, could imagine, that the most violent local prejudices would cease so soon; and that men, who came from the different parts of the continent, strongly disposed by the habits of education to despise and quarrel with each other, would instantly become but one patriotic band of brothers? Or who, that was not on the spot, can trace the steps by which such a wonderful revolution has been effected, and such a glorious period put to all our warlike toils?

It is universally acknowledged that the enlarged prospects of happiness, opened by the confirmation of our independence and sovereignty, almost exceed the power of description. And shall not the brave men, who have contributed so essentially to these inestimable acquisitions, retiring victorious from the field of war to the field of agriculture, participate in all the blessings which have been obtained? In such a republic, who will exclude them from the rights of citizens, and the fruits of their labor? In such a country, so happily circumstanced, the pursuits of commerce and the cultivation of the soil will unfold to industry the certain road to competence. To those hardy soldiers, who are actuated by the spirit of adventure, the fisheries will afford ample and profitable employment;

and the extensive and fertile regions of the West will yield a most happy asylum to those who, fond of domestic enjoyment, are seeking for personal independence. Nor is it possible to conceive that any one of the United States will prefer a national bankruptcy, and a dissolution of the Union, to a compliance with the requisitions of Congress, and the payment of its just debts; so that the officers and soldiers may expect considerable assistance, in recommencing their civil occupations, from the sums due to them from the public, which must and will most inevitably be paid.

In order to effect this desirable purpose, and to remove the prejudices which may have taken possession of the minds of any of the good people of the States, it is earnestly recommended to all the troops that, with strong attachments to the Union, they should carry with them into civil society the most conciliating dispositions, and that they should prove themselves not less virtuous and useful as citizens than they have been persevering and victorious as soldiers. What though there should be some envious individuals, who are unwilling to pay the debt the public has contracted, or to yield the tribute due to merit; yet let such unworthy treatment produce no invectives, nor any instance of intemperate conduct. Let it be remembered that the unbiased voice of the free citizens of the United States has promised the just reward and given the merited applause. Let it be known and remembered that the reputation of the federal armies is established beyond the reach of malevolence; and let a consciousness of their achievements and fame still incite the men who composed them to honorable actions; under the persuasion that the private virtues of economy, prudence and industry will not be less amiable in civil life than the more splendid qualities of valor, perseverance and enterprise were in the field. Every one may rest assured that much, very much of the future happiness of the officers and men will depend upon the wise and manly conduct which shall be adopted by them when they are mingled with the great body of the community. And although the general has so frequently given it as his opinion in the most public and explicit manner that, unless the principles of the federal government were properly supported, and the powers of the Union increased, the honor, dignity and justice of the nation would be lost forever; yet he cannot help repeating on this occasion so interesting a sentiment, and leaving it as his last injunction to every officer and every soldier, who may view the subject in the same serious point of light, to add his best endeavors to those of his worthy fellow-citizens toward effecting these great and valuable purposes, on which our very existence as a nation so materially depends.

The commander-in-chief conceives little is now wanting to enable the soldiers to change the military character into that of the citizen, but that steady and decent tenor of behavior which has generally distinguished, not only the army under his immediate command, but the different detachments and separate armies through the course of the war. From their good sense and prudence he anticipates the happiest consequences, and while he congratulates them on the glorious occasion which renders their services in the field no longer necessary, he wishes to express the strong obligations he feels himself under for the assistance he has received from every class and in every instance. He presents his thanks in the most serious and affectionate manner to the general officers, as well for their counsel on many interesting occasions, as for their ardor in promoting the success of the plans he had adopted; to the commandants of regiments and corps, and to the other officers, for their great zeal and attention in carrying his orders promptly into execution; to the staff, for their alacrity and exactness in performing the duties of their several departments; and to the non-commissioned officers and private soldiers, for their extraordinary patience and suffering, as well as their invincible fortitude in action. To the various branches of the army the General takes this last and solemn opportunity of professing his inviolable attachment and friendship. He wishes more than bare professions were in his power; that he were really able to be useful to them all in future life. He flatters himself, however, they will do him the justice to believe, that whatever could with propriety be attempted by him has been done.

And being now to conclude these his last public orders, to take his ultimate leave in a short time of the military character, and to bid a final adieu to the armies he has so long had the honor to command, he can only again offer in their behalf his recommendations to their grateful country, and his prayers to the God of armies. May ample justice be done them here, and may the choicest of Heaven's favors, both here and hereafter, attend those who, under the Divine auspices, have secured innumerable blessings for others. With these wishes and his benediction, the commander-in-chief is about to retire from service. The curtain of separation will soon be drawn, and the military scene to him will be closed forever.

X.

FAREWELL ADDRESS TO THE PEOPLE OF THE UNITED STATES.

WASHINGTON was chosen first President of the United States, and at the end of his term he was again chosen. When his second term drew near its close, he refused to be a candidate for reëlection, and six months before he was to leave the President's chair he issued the following farewell address, September 17, 1796.

FRIENDS AND FELLOW-CITIZENS: The period for a new election of a citizen, to administer the executive government of the United States, being not far distant, and the time actually arrived when your thoughts must be employed in designating the person who is to be clothed with that important trust, it appears to me proper, especially as it may conduce to a more distinct expression of the public voice, that I should now apprise you of the resolution I have formed, to decline being considered among the number of those out of whom a choice is to be made.

I beg you, at the same time, to do me the justice to be assured, that this resolution has not been taken without a strict regard to all the considerations appertaining to the relation which binds a dutiful citizen to his country; and that, in withdrawing the tender of service, which silence in my situation might imply, I am influenced by no diminution of zeal for your future interest; no deficiency of grateful respect for your past kindness; but am supported by a full conviction that the step is compatible with both.

The acceptance of, and continuance hitherto in, the office to which your suffrages have twice called me, have been a uniform sacrifice of inclination to the opinion of duty, and to a deference for what appeared to be your desire. I constantly hoped that it would have been much earlier in my power, consistently with motives which I was not at liberty to disregard, to return to that retirement from which I had been reluctantly drawn. The strength of my inclination to do this, previous to the last election, had even led to the preparation of an address to declare it to you; but mature reflection on the then perplexed and critical posture of our affairs with foreign nations, and the unanimous advice of persons entitled to my confidence, impelled me to abandon the idea.

I rejoice that the state of your concerns, external as well as internal, no longer renders the pursuit of inclination incompatible with the sentiment of duty or propriety; and am persuaded, whatever partiality may be retained for my services, that, in the present circumstances of our country, you will not disapprove my determination to retire.

The impressions with which I first undertook the arduous trust were explained on the proper occasion. In the discharge of this trust I will only say that I have with good intentions contributed toward the organization and administration of the government the best exertions of which a very fallible judgment was capable. Not unconscious in the outset of the inferiority of my qualifications, experience in my own eyes, perhaps still more in the eyes of others, has strengthened the motives to diffidence of myself; and every day the increasing weight of years admonishes me more and more that the shade of retirement is as necessary to me as it will be welcome. Satisfied that, if any circumstances have given peculiar value to my services, they were temporary, I have the consolation to believe that, while choice and prudence invite me to quit the political scene, patriotism does not forbid it.

In looking forward to the moment which is intended to terminate the career of my public life, my feelings do not permit me to suspend the deep acknowledgment of that debt of gratitude which I owe to my beloved country for the many honors it has conferred upon me; still more for the steadfast confidence with which it has supported me; and for the opportunities I have thence enjoyed of manifesting my inviolable attachment by services faithful and persevering, though in usefulness unequal to my zeal. If benefits have resulted to our country from these services, let it always be remembered to your praise, and as an instructive example in our annals, that under circumstances in which the passions, agitated in every direction, were liable to mislead, amidst appearances sometimes dubious, vicissitudes of fortune often discouraging, in situations in which not unfrequently want of success has countenanced the spirit of criticism, the constancy of your support was the essential prop of the efforts, and a guaranty of the plans by which they were effected. Profoundly penetrated with this idea, I shall carry it with me to my grave, as a strong incitement to unceasing vows that Heaven may continue to you the choicest tokens of its beneficence; that your union and brotherly affection may be perpetual; that the free constitution, which is the work of your hands, may be sacredly maintained; that its administration in every department may be stamped with wisdom and virtue; that, in fine, the happiness of the people of these States, under the auspices of liberty, may be made complete, by so careful a preservation and so prudent a use of this blessing, as will acquire to them the glory of recommending it to the applause, the affection, and adoption of every nation which is yet a stranger to it.

Here, perhaps, I ought to stop. But a solicitude for your welfare, which cannot end but with my life, and the apprehension of danger natural to that solicitude, urge me, on an occasion like the present, to offer to your solemn contemplation, and to recommend to your frequent review, some sentiments, which are the result of much reflection, of no inconsiderable observation, and which appear to me all-important to the permanency of your felicity as a people. These will be offered to you with the more freedom, as you can only see in them the disinterested warnings of a parting friend, who can possibly have no personal motive to bias his counsel. Nor can I forget, as an encouragement to it, your indulgent reception of my sentiments on a former and not dissimilar occasion.

Interwoven as is the love of liberty with every ligament of your hearts, no recommendation of mine is necessary to fortify or confirm the attachment.

The unity of government, which constitutes you one people, is also now dear to you. It is justly so; for it is a main pillar in the edifice of your real independence, the support of your tranquillity at home, your peace abroad; of your safety; of your prosperity; of that very liberty which you so highly prize. But as it is easy to foresee that from different causes and from different quarters much pains will be taken, many artifices employed, to weaken in your minds the conviction of this truth; as this is the point in your political fortress against which the batteries of internal and external enemies will be most constantly and actively (though often covertly and insidiously) directed, it is of infinite moment that you should properly estimate the immense value of your national union to your collective and individual happiness; that you should cherish a cordial, habitual, and immovable attachment to it; accustoming yourselves to think and speak of it as of the palladium of your political safety and prosperity: watching for its preservation with jealous anxiety; discountenancing whatever may suggest even a suspicion that it can in any event be abandoned; and indignantly frowning upon the first dawning of every attempt to alienate any portion of our country from the rest, or to enfeeble the sacred ties which now link together the various parts.

For this you have every inducement of sympathy and interest. Citizens, by birth or choice, of a common country, that country has a right to concentrate your affections. The name of America, which belongs to you, in your national capacity, must always exalt the just pride of patriotism, more than any appellation derived from local discriminations. With slight shades of difference, you have the same religion, manners, habits, and political principles. You have in a common cause fought and triumphed together; the independence and liberty you possess are the work of joint counsels and joint efforts, of common dangers, sufferings and successes.

But these considerations, however powerfully they address themselves to your sensibility, are greatly outweighed by those which apply more immediately to your interest. Here every portion of our country finds the most commanding motives for carefully guarding and preserving the union of the whole.

The North, in an unrestrained intercourse with the

South, protected by the equal laws of a common government, finds in the productions of the latter great additional resources of maritime and commercial enterprise and precious materials of manufacturing industry. The South in the same intercourse, benefiting by the agency of the North, sees its agriculture grow and its commerce expand. Turning partly into its own channels the seamen of the North, it finds its particular navigation invigorated; and, while it contributes in different ways to nourish and increase the general mass of the national navigation, it looks forward to the protection of a maritime strength, to which itself is unequally adapted. The East, in a like intercourse with the West, already finds, and in the progressive improvement of interior communications by land and water will more and more find, a valuable vent for the commodities which it brings from abroad, or manufactures at home. The West derives from the East supplies requisite to its growth and comfort, and, what is perhaps of still greater consequence, it must of necessity owe the secure enjoyment of indispensable outlets for its own productions to the weight, influence, and the future maritime strength of the Atlantic side of the Union, directed by an indissoluble community of interest as one nation. Any other tenure by which the West can hold this essential advantage, whether derived from its own separate strength or from an apostate and unnatural connection with any foreign power, must be intrinsically precarious.

While, then, every part of our country thus feels an immediate and particular interest in union, all the parts combined cannot fail to find in the united mass of means and efforts greater strength, greater resource, proportionably greater security from external danger, a less frequent interruption of their peace by foreign nations, and, what is of inestimable value, they must derive from union an exemption from those broils and wars between themselves, which so frequently afflict neighboring countries not tied together by the same governments, which their own rivalships alone would be sufficient to produce, but which opposite foreign alliances, attachments, and intrigues would stimulate and embitter. Hence, likewise, they will avoid the necessity of those overgrown military establishments which, under any form of government, are inauspicious to liberty, and which are to be regarded as particularly hostile to republican liberty. In this sense it is that your union ought to be considered as a main prop of your liberty, and that the love of the one ought to endear to you the preservation of the other.

These considerations speak a persuasive language to every reflecting and virtuous mind, and exhibit the continuance of the Union as a primary object of patriotic desire. Is there a doubt whether a common government can embrace so large a sphere? Let experience solve it. To listen to mere speculation in such a case were criminal. We are authorized to hope that a proper organization of the whole, with the auxiliary agency of governments for the respective subdivisions, will afford a happy issue to the experiment. It is well worth a fair and full experiment. With such powerful and obvious motives to union, affecting all parts of our country, while experience shall not have demonstrated its impracticability, there will always be reason to distrust the patriotism of those who in any quarter may endeavor to weaken its bands.

In contemplating the causes which may disturb our Union, it occurs as a matter of serious concern, that any ground should have been furnished for characterizing parties by geographical discriminations Northern and Southern, Atlantic and Western; whence designing men may endeavor to excite a belief that there is a real difference of local interests and views. One of the expedients of party to acquire influence, within particular districts, is to misrepresent the opinions and aims of other districts. You cannot shield yourselves too much against the jealousies and heart-burnings which spring from these misrepresentations; they tend to render alien to each other those who ought to be bound together by fraternal affection. The inhabitants of our western country have lately had a useful lesson on this head; they have seen, in the negotiation by the executive, and in the unanimous ratification by the senate, of the treaty with Spain, and in the universal satisfaction at that event throughout the United States, a decisive proof how unfounded were the suspicions propagated among them of a policy in the general government and in the Atlantic States unfriendly to their interests in regard to the Mississippi; they have been witnesses to the formation of two treaties, that with Great Britain and that with Spain, which secure to them everything they could desire, in respect to our foreign relations, towards confirming their prosperity. Will it not be their wisdom to rely for the preservation of these advantages on the Union by which they were procured? Will they not henceforth be deaf to those advisers, if such there are, who would sever them from their brethren and connect them with aliens?

To the efficacy and permanency of your union, a

government for the whole is indispensable. No alliances, however strict, between the parts can be an adequate substitute; they must inevitably experience the infractions and interruptions which all alliances in all times have experienced. Sensible of this momentous truth, you have improved upon your first essay, by the adoption of a constitution of government better calculated than your former for an intimate union, and for the efficacious management of your common concerns. This government, the offspring of our own choice, uninfluenced and unawed, adopted upon full investigation and mature deliberation, completely free in its principles, in the distribution of its powers, uniting security with energy, and containing within itself a provision for its own amendment, has a just claim to your confidence and your support. Respect for its authority, compliance with its laws, acquiescence in its measures, are duties enjoined by the fundamental maxims of true Liberty. The basis of our political systems is the right of the people to make and to alter their constitutions of government. But the constitution which at any time exists, till changed by an explicit and authentic act of the whole people, is sacredly obligatory upon all. The very idea of the power and the right of the people to establish government presupposes the duty of every individual to obey the established government.

All obstructions to the execution of the laws, all combinations and associations, under whatever plausible character, with the real design to direct, control, counteract, or awe the regular deliberation and action of the constituted authorities, are destructive of this fundamental principle, and of fatal tendency. They serve to organize faction, to give it an artificial and extraordinary force; to put in the place of the delegated will of the nation, the will of a party, often a small but artful and enterprising minority of the community; and, according to the alternate triumphs of different parties, to make the public administration the mirror of the ill-concerted and incongruous projects of fashion, rather than the organs of consistent and wholesome plans digested by common councils, and modified by mutual interests.

However combinations or associations of the above description may now and then answer popular ends, they are likely, in the course of time and things, to become potent engines, by which cunning, ambitious, and unprincipled men will be enabled to subvert the power of the people, and to usurp for themselves the reins of government; destroying afterwards the very engines which have lifted them to unjust dominion.

Towards the preservation of your government, and the permanency of your present happy state, it is requisite, not only that you steadily discountenance irregular oppositions to its acknowledged authority, but also that you resist with care the spirit of innovation upon its principles, however specious the pretexts. One method of assault may be to effect, in the forms of the constitution, alterations, which will impair the energy of the system, and thus to undermine what cannot be directly overthrown. In all the changes to which you may be invited, remember that time and habit are at least as necessary to fix the true character of governments as of other human institutions; that experience is the surest standard by which to test the real tendency of the existing constitution of a country; that facility in changes, upon the credit of mere hypothesis and opinion, exposes to perpetual change, from the endless variety of hypothesis and opinion; and remember, especially, that, for the efficient management of your common interests, in a country so extensive as ours, a government of as much vigor as is consistent with the perfect security of liberty is indispensable. Liberty itself will find in such a government, with powers properly distributed and adjusted, its surest guardian. It is, indeed, little else than a name, where the government is too feeble to withstand the enterprises of faction, to confine each member of the society within the limits prescribed by the laws, and to maintain all in the secure and tranquil enjoyment of the rights of person and property.

I have already intimated to you the danger of parties in the State, with particular reference to the founding of them on geographical discrimination. Let me now take a more comprehensive view, and warn you in the most solemn manner against the baneful effects of the spirit of party, generally.

This spirit, unfortunately, is inseparable from our nature, having its root in the strongest passions of the human mind. It exists under different shapes in all governments, more or less stifled, controlled, or repressed; but in those of the popular form it is seen in its greatest rankness, and is truly their worst enemy.

The alternate domination of one faction over another, sharpened by the spirit of revenge, natural to party dissension, which in different ages and countries has perpetrated the most horrid enormities, is itself a frightful despotism. But this leads at length to a more formal and permanent despotism. The disorders and miseries which result, gradually incline the minds of men to seek security and repose in the absolute power of an individual; and sooner or later the chief of some prevailing faction, more able or more fortunate than his competitors, turns this disposition to the purposes of his own elevation, on the ruins of public liberty.

Without looking forward to an extremity of this kind (which nevertheless ought not to be entirely out of sight), the common and continued mischiefs of the spirit of party are sufficient to make it the interest and duty of a wise people to discourage and restrain it.

It serves always to distract the public councils, and enfeeble the public administration. It agitates the community with ill-founded jealousies and false alarms; kindles the animosity of one part against another, foments occasionally riot and insurrection. It opens the doors to foreign influence and corruption, which find a facilitated access to the government itself through the channels of party passions. Thus the policy and the will of one country are subjected to the policy and will of another.

There is an opinion, that parties in free countries are useful checks upon the administration of the government, and serve to keep alive the spirit of liberty. This within certain limits is probably true, and in governments of a monarchical cast, patriotism may look with indulgence, if not with favor, upon the spirit of party. But in those of the popular character, in governments purely elective, it is a spirit not to be encouraged. From their natural tendency, it is certain there will always be enough of that spirit for every salutary purpose. And there being constant danger of excess, the effort ought to be, by force of public opinion to mitigate and assuage it. A fire not to be quenched, it demands a uniform vigilance to prevent its bursting into a flame, lest, instead of warming, it should consume.

It is important, likewise, that the habits of thinking in a free country should inspire caution, in those intrusted with its administration, to confine themselves within their respective constitutional spheres, avoiding in the exercise of the powers of one department to encroach upon another. The spirit of encroachment tends to consolidate the powers of all the departments in one, and thus to create, whatever the form of government, a real despotism. A just estimate of that love of power, and proneness to abuse it, which predominates in the human heart, is sufficient to satisfy us of the truth of this position. The necessity of reciprocal checks in the exercise of political power, by dividing and distributing it into different depositories, and constituting each the guardian of the public weal against invasions by the others, has been evinced by experiments ancient and modern, some of them in our country and under our own eyes. To preserve them must be as necessary as to institute them. If, in the opinion of the people, the distribution or modification of the constitutional powers be in any particular wrong, let it be corrected by an amendment in the way which the Constitution designates. But let there be no change by usurpation; for, though this, in one instance, may be the instrument of good, it is the customary weapon by which free governments are destroyed. The precedent must always greatly overbalance in permanent evil any partial or transient benefit which the use can at any time yield.

Of all the dispositions and habits which lead to political prosperity, religion and morality are indispensable supports. In vain would that man claim the tribute of patriotism, who should labor to subvert these great pillars of human happiness, these firmest props of the duties of men and citizens. The mere politician equally with the pious man ought to respect and to cherish them. A volume could not trace all their connections with private and public felicity. Let it simply be asked, Where is the security for property, for reputation, for life, if the sense of religious obligation desert the oaths, which are the instruments of investigation in courts of justice? And let us with caution indulge the supposition, that morality can be maintained without religion. Whatever may be conceded to the influence of refined education on minds of peculiar structure, reason and experience both forbid us to expect, that national morality can prevail in exclusion of religious principle.

It is substantially true that virtue or morality is a necessary spring of popular government. The rule, indeed, extends with more or less force to every species of free government. Who, that is a sincere friend to it, can look with indifference upon attempts to shake the foundation of the fabric?

Promote, then, as an object of primary importance, institutions for the general diffusion of knowledge. In proportion as the structure of a government gives force to public opinion, it is essential that public opinion should be enlightened.

As a very important source of strength and security, cherish public credit. One method of preserving it is, to use it as sparingly as possible; avoiding occasions of expense by cultivating peace, but remembering also that timely disbursements to prepare for danger frequently prevent much greater disbursements to repel it; avoiding likewise the accumulation of debt, not only by shunning occasions of expense, but by vigorous exertion in time of peace to discharge the debts, which unavoidable wars may have occasioned, not ungenerously throwing upon posterity the burden which we ourselves ought to bear. The execution of these maxims belongs to your representatives, but it is necessary that public opinion should co-operate. To facilitate to them the performance of their duty it is essential that you should practically bear in mind, that towards the payment of debts there must be revenue; that to have revenue there must be taxes; that no taxes can be devised which are not more or less inconvenient and unpleasant; that the intrinsic embarrassment, inseparable from the selection of the proper objects (which is always a choice of difficulties), ought to be a decisive motive for a candid construction of the conduct of the government in making it, and for a spirit of acquiescence in the measures for obtaining revenue which the public exigencies may at any time dictate.

Observe good faith and justice towards all nations; cultivate peace and harmony with all. Religion and morality enjoin this conduct; and can it be, that good policy does not equally enjoin it? It will be worthy of a free, enlightened, and at no distant period a great nation, to give to mankind the magnanimous and too novel example of a people always guided by an exalted justice and benevolence. Who can doubt that in the course of time and things, the fruits of such a plan would richly repay any temporary advantages, which might be lost by a steady adherence to it? Can it be that Providence has not connected the permanent felicity of a nation with its virtue? The experiment, at least, is recommended by every sentiment which ennobles human nature. Alas! is it rendered impossible by its vices?

In the execution of such a plan, nothing is more essential than that permanent, inveterate antipathies against particular nations, and passionate attachments for others, should be excluded; and that, in place of them, just and amicable feelings towards all should be cultivated. The nation which indulges towards another an habitual hatred, or an habitual fondness, is in some degree a slave. It is a slave to its animosity or to its affection, either of which is sufficient to lead it astray from its duty and its interest. Antipathy in one nation against another disposes each more readily to offer insult and injury, to lay hold of slight causes of umbrage, and to be haughty and intractable when accidental or trifling occasions of dispute occur. Hence, frequent collisions, obstinate, envenomed, and bloody contests. The nation, prompted by ill-will and resentment, sometimes impels to war the government, contrary to the best calculations of policy. The government sometimes participates in the national propensity, and adopts through passion what reason would reject; at other times, it makes the animosity of the nation subservient to projects of hostility instigated by pride, ambition, and other sinister and pernicious motives. The peace often, sometimes perhaps the liberty, of nations has been the victim.

So likewise, a passionate attachment of one nation for another produces a variety of evils. Sympathy for the favorite nation, facilitating the illusion of an imaginary common interest in cases where no real common interest exists, and infusing into one the enmities of the other, betrays the former into a participation in the quarrels and wars of the latter, without adequate inducement or justification. It leads also to concessions to the favorite nation of privileges denied to others, which is apt doubly to injure the nation making the concessions, by unnecessarily parting with what ought to have been retained, and by exciting jealousy, ill-will, and a disposition to retaliate, in the parties from whom equal privileges are withheld. And it gives to ambitious, corrupted, or deluded citizens (who devote themselves to the favorite nation), facility to betray or sacrifice the interests of their own country, without odium, sometimes even with popularity; gilding with the appearances of a virtuous sense of obligation, a commendable deference for public opinion, or a laudable zeal for public good, the base or foolish compliances of ambition, corruption, or infatuation.

As avenues to foreign influence in innumerable ways such attachments are particularly alarming to the truly enlightened and independent patriot. How many opportunities do they afford to tamper with domestic factions, to practise the arts of seduction, to mislead public opinion, to influence or awe the public councils! Such an attachment of a small or weak, towards a great and powerful nation, dooms the former to be the satellite of the latter.

Against the insidious wiles of foreign influence (I conjure you to believe me, fellow-citizens), the jealousy of a free people ought to be constantly awake, since history and experience prove that foreign influence is one of the most baneful foes of republican government. But that jealousy, to be useful, must be impartial; else it becomes the instrument of the very influence to be avoided, instead of a defence against it.

Excessive partiality for one foreign nation, and excessive dislike of another, cause those whom they actuate to see danger only on one side, and serve to veil and even second the arts of influence on the other. Real patriots who may resist the intrigues of the favorite, are liable to become suspected and odious; while its tools and dupes usurp the applause and confidence of the purpose, to surrender their interests.

The great rule of conduct for us, in regard to foreign nations, is, in extending our commercial relations, to have with them as little political connection as possible. So far as we have already formed engagements, let them be fulfilled with perfect good faith. Here let us stop.

Europe has a set of primary interests, which to us have none, or a very remote relation. Hence she must be engaged in frequent controversies, the causes of which are essentially foreign to our concerns. Hence, therefore, it must be unwise in us to implicate ourselves, by artificial ties, in the ordinary vicissitudes of her politics, or the ordinary combinations and collisions of her friendships or enmities.

Our detached and distant situation invites and enables us to pursue a different course. If we remain one people, under an efficient government, the period is not far off when we may defy material injury from external annoyance; when we may take such an attitude as will cause the neutrality, we may at any time resolve upon, to be scrupulously respected; when belligerent nations, under the impossibility of making acquisitions upon us, will not lightly hazard the giving us provocation; when we may choose peace or war, as our interest, guided by justice, shall counsel.

Why forego the advantages of so peculiar a situation? Why quit our own to stand upon foreign ground? Why, by interweaving our destiny with that of any part of Europe, entangle our peace and prosperity in the toils of European ambition, rivalship, interest, humor, or caprice?

It is our true policy to steer clear of permanent alliances with any portion of the foreign world; so far, I mean, as we are now at liberty to do it; for let me not be understood as capable of patronizing infidelity to existing engagements. I hold the maxim no less applicable to public than to private affairs, that honesty is always the best policy. I repeat it, therefore, let those engagements be observed in their genuine sense. But, in my opinion, it is unnecessary and would be unwise to extend them.

Taking care always to keep ourselves, by suitable establishments, on a respectable defensive posture, we may safely trust to temporary alliances for extraordinary emergencies.

Harmony, liberal intercourse with all nations, are recommended by policy, humanity, and interest. But even our commercial policy should hold an equal and impartial hand; neither seeking nor granting exclusive favors or preferences; consulting the natural course of things; diffusing and diversifying by gentle means the streams of commerce, but forcing nothing; establishing with powers so disposed, in order to give trade a stable course, to define the rights of our merchants, and to enable the government to support them, conventional rules of intercourse, the best that present circumstances and mutual opinion will permit, but temporary, and liable to be from time to time abandoned or varied, as experience and circumstances shall dictate; constantly keeping in view, that it is folly in one nation to look for disinterested favors from another; that it must pay with a portion of its independence for whatever it may accept under that character; that, by such acceptance, it may place itself in the condition of having given equivalents for nominal favors, and yet of being reproached with ingratitude for not giving more. There can be no greater error than to expect or calculate upon real favors from nation to nation. It is an illusion, which experience must cure, which a just pride ought to discard.

In offering to you, my countrymen, these counsels of an old and affectionate friend, I dare not hope they will make the strong and lasting impression I could wish; that they will control the usual current of the passions, or prevent our nation from running the course which has hitherto marked the destiny of nations. But, if I may even flatter myself that they may be productive of some partial benefit, some occasional good; that they may now and then recur to moderate the fury of party spirit, to warn against the mischiefs of foreign intrigue, to guard against the impostures of pretended patriotism; this hope will be a full recompense for the solicitude for your welfare, by which they have been dictated.

How far in the discharge of my official duties I have been guided by the principles which have been delineated, the public records and other evidences of my conduct must witness to you and to the world. To myself, the assurance of my own conscience is, that I have at least believed myself to be guided by them.

In relation to the still subsisting war in Europe, my proclamation of the 22d of April, 1793, is the index of my plan. Sanctioned by your approving voice, and by that of your Representatives in both Houses of Congress, the spirit of that measure has continually governed me, uninfluenced by any attempts to deter or divert me from it.

After deliberate examination, with the aid of the best lights I could obtain, I was well satisfied that our country, under all the circumstances of the case, had a right to take, and was bound in duty and interest to take, a neutral position. Having taken it, I determined, as far as should depend upon me, to maintain it, with moderation, perseverance and firmness.

The considerations which respect the right to hold this conduct, it is not necessary on this occasion to detail. I will only observe, that, according to my understanding of the matter, that right, so far from being denied by any of the belligerent powers, has been virtually admitted by all.

The duty of holding a neutral conduct may be inferred, without anything more, from the obligation which justice and humanity impose on every nation, in cases in which it is free to act, to maintain inviolate the relations of peace and amity towards other nations.

The inducements of interest for observing that conduct will best be referred to your own reflections and experience. With me a predominant motive has been to endeavor to gain time to our country to settle and mature its yet recent institutions, and to progress without interruption to that degree of strength and consistency which is necessary to give it, humanly speaking, the command of its own fortunes.

Though, in reviewing the incidents of my administration, I am unconscious of intentional error, I am nevertheless too sensible of my defects not to think it probable that I may have committed many errors.

Whatever they may be, I fervently beseech the Almighty to avert or mitigate the evils to which they may tend. I shall also carry with me the hope that my country will never cease to view them with indulgence; and that, after forty-five years of my life dedicated to its service with an upright zeal, the faults of incompetent abilities will be consigned to oblivion, as myself must soon be to the mansions of rest.

Relying on its kindness in this as in other things, and actuated by that fervent love towards it, which is so natural to a man who views in it the native soil of himself and his progenitors for several generations, I anticipate with pleasing expectation that retreat, in which I promise myself to realize, without alloy, the sweet enjoyment of partaking, in the midst of my fellow-citizens, the benign influence of good laws under a free government, the ever favorite object of my heart, and the happy reward, as I trust, of our mutual cares, labors, and dangers.

GEORGE WASHINGTON.

EVENTS IN THE LIFE OF GEORGE WASHINGTON.

Born	February 22, 1732.
Father dies	April 12, 1743.
Leaves school	Autumn, 1747.
Goes on his first surveying expedition .	March, 1748.
Commissioned adjutant-general, with rank of major	1751.
Sails for the West Indies with his brother Lawrence	September, 1751.
Lawrence dies, leaving George executor of his will	1752.
Is sent on a mission to the Ohio Country .	November 31, 1753.
Commissioned lieutenant-colonel . .	1754.
Fights at Great Meadows	July 3, 1754.
Is appointed aid-de-camp to General Braddock	1755.
Braddock's defeat	July 9, 1755.
Is elected representative to the House of Burgesses	1758.
Marries Mrs. Martha Custis . . .	January 6, 1759.
Is a member of the first Continental Congress	1774.
Is a member of the second Continental Congress	1775.
Appointed Commander-in-Chief of the American armies	June 15, 1775.
Takes command at Cambridge . .	July 3, 1775.
Siege of Boston raised	March, 1776.
Declaration of Independence . . .	July 4, 1776.
Battle of Long Island	August 22, 1776.
Battle of White Plains	October 28, 1776.
Fort Washington abandoned . . .	November 16, 1776.
Battle of Trenton	November 16, 1776.

Battle of Princeton	January 3, 1777.
Flag of stars and stripes adopted by Congress	June 14, 1777.
Battle of the Brandywine	September 10, 1777.
Battle of Germantown	October 4, 1777.
Ratification of Treaty with France . .	May 2, 1778.
Battle of Monmouth Court House . .	June 28, 1778.
Arrival of French fleet	July, 1778.
Arnold's treason	September, 1780.
Execution of André	October 2, 1780.
Cornwallis's surrender at Yorktown . .	October 19, 1781.
Takes leave of the army	November 2, 1783.
Resigns his commission	December 23, 1783.
Presides at the Constitutional Convention,	1787.
Is chosen first President of the United States	1789.
Inaugurated	April 30, 1789.
His mother dies	August, 1789.
Makes a tour through the Northern States,	1789.
Makes a tour through the Southern States,	1790.
Chosen for second term	1793.
Issues proclamation of neutrality . .	April 22, 1793.
Nominates John Jay as envoy extraordinary to Great Britain	April 16, 1794.
Signs the Jay Treaty	August 18, 1795.
Issues a Farewell Address to the people of the United States	September 15, 1796.
Retires from the Presidency	March 4, 1797.
Is nominated Commander-in-Chief of the armies of the United States	July 2, 1798.
Dies	December 18, 1799.

www.ingramcontent.com/pod-product-compliance
Lightning Source LLC
Chambersburg PA
CBHW030546270326
41927CB00008B/1540
* 9 7 8 3 7 4 4 7 0 0 5 2 8 *